Galatians

Unlocking the Power of Paul's Hyper-Grace Message

Don Keathley

TWS | THE WRITER'S SOCIETY PUBLISHING

Copyright © 2023 by Don Keathley

All rights reserved.

No part of this book may be reproduced in any form or by any electronic or mechanical means, including information storage and retrieval systems, without written permission from the author, except for the use of brief quotations in a book review.

To request permissions, contact TWS Publishing at www.thewriterssociety.online

New King James Version®, Copyright© 1982, Thomas Nelson. All rights reserved.

Paperback: ISBN 978-1-961180-22-2

TWS Publishing
Lodi, CA
www.thewriterssociety.online

Contents

Introduction ... vii

Part One
Unpacking The Gospel Of Grace

1. PAUL'S GOSPEL OF GRACE ... 3
   Understanding Paul's Unshakable Authority ... 3
   The True Meaning of 'Sin' Unveiled ... 5
   Confronting Counterfeit Gospels ... 8
   Rediscovering the Simplicity of Grace ... 11

2. PAUL'S JOURNEY TO RADICAL GRACE BEGINS ... 13
   Leaving Religion for Radical Grace ... 13
   Discovering the Christ Within ... 17
   Maturing in Revelation During Paul's Desert Journey ... 21
   Embracing Four Profound Shifts in Grace ... 23

3. THE TRANSFORMATION OF GRACE ... 28
   Paul's 14-Year Transformation: A Time of Preparation ... 29
   A Bold Political Move: Paul's Meeting with Jerusalem Leaders ... 30
   Clash of Titans: Paul, James, and John ... 32
   The Influence of Modern-Day Judaizers: Calvinists & Arminians ... 36
   The Unveiled Gospel of Grace: All Included ... 38

4. GRACE UNLEASHED: OVERCOMING HYPOCRISY AND RELIGION ... 40
   When Grace Confronts Law: Exposing Peter's Hypocrisy ... 41
   Righteousness Through Christ's Faith ... 45
   Freedom from Condemnation: No Judgment in Christ ... 47

Grace vs. Religion: Unveiling the Liberating Gospel — 49
Religion's Veil Over Grace — 52
The Unchanging Truth of God's Goodness: Love That Never Fails — 54

5. GRACE IN ACTION — 56
Law and Grace on a Collision Course: A Lethal Combination — 56
Abraham's Faith: A Blueprint for Trusting God — 60
Mary & Martha: The Choice of Rest or Striving — 64
Embracing the Completed Work: It's a Done Deal! — 66

6. BREAKING FREE WITH GRACE — 68
Escaping the Heavy Burden of the Law — 69
The Church's Shift: Departing from a Christ-Centered Gospel — 69
Sickness, Death, and Poverty: The Curse of the Law — 71
Our Divine Inheritance: The Blessing of Abraham — 74

7. THE TRANSFORMATIVE POWER OF WORDS — 77
Reclaiming the Language of Grace — 78
Confession: Agreeing With God — 79
Belief: The Effortless Response to Divine Revelation — 83
Faith: Trusting in God's Unlimited Power — 85
Receiving: Embracing Our Divine Inheritance — 88
A Legacy of Grace: Unlocking God's Covenant with Abraham — 88
Moving Forward: The Path to Sonship in Grace — 91

Part Two
Manifested Sonship: The Grace Journey Continues

8. EMBRACING SONSHIP AND AUTHORITY ... 95
   Unveiling the Mystery: Christ in You ... 96
   From Child Heirs to Mature Sons ... 97
   The Shift from Servants to Manifested Sons ... 99
   The Divine Transition: Becoming a Manifested Sonship ... 104
   The Power of Adoption ... 108

9. UNVEILING SONSHIP'S FOUR STAGES ... 109
   The Crucible of Sonship: Growth and Patience ... 109
   Embracing Divine Discipline ... 111
   Stage One - *NEIPOS*: Spiritual Babyhood ... 114
   Stage Two - *PAIDION*: Childlike Sons ... 116
   Stage Three - TEKNON: The Teenage Phase ... 119
   Stage Four - HUIOS: The Maturity of Manifested Sonship ... 123

10. BREAKING RELIGIOUS BARRIERS ... 128
    Shattering False Perceptions: Discovering the True Nature of God ... 128
    Embracing Freedom: Liberating Your Faith from Religious Rituals ... 132
    Grace vs. Religion: Zealous Pursuit of Truth ... 133
    Revelation Maturing: Growing in the Light of Grace ... 137

11. BREAKING RELIGIOUS CHAINS: FREEDOM IN GRACE ... 140
    Law vs. Grace: An Unveiling Analogy ... 140
    Ishmael and the Flesh: Striving vs. Trusting ... 142
    Embracing Grace: Liberation from Religious Obligation ... 143
    Unlocking Freedom: Five Essential Questions ... 145

12. UNMASKING YOUR TRUE IDENTITY	153
Subverting the Identity Thieves	155
Firmly Rooted Identity: A Foundation for Purpose	156
Firmly Rooted Identity: A Foundation For Purpose	158
Defending, Embracing, and Thriving in Your Identity	160
13. LIVING IN THE SPIRIT REALM	165
Soul vs. Spirit: Freedom from the Law	166
The Battle Within: Flesh vs. Spirit	169
Unveiling the Unseen Realm: A New Awakening	170
Tuning Into Divine Frequencies	174
Transitioning to a New Dimension of Reality	177
14. SPIRIT LED DECISION MAKING	181
Paul's Urgent Plea: Restoring Others with Compassion	182
Navigating Life's Crossroads in the Spirit	185
Seven Vital Questions for a Purposeful Journey	187
About the Author	197
Also by Don Keathley	199

Introduction

This book is the first in a series where we explore Paul's epistles, including Galatians, Ephesians, Philippians, and Colossians. We'll dive deep into these writings to understand what Paul teaches about the finished work of the cross and our inheritance in Christ.

The goal is to understand what Paul said and why he said it, connecting his words to our world. As we progress, expect fresh insights, hidden truths, and growth in grace and knowledge.

Galatians, the initial focus of our exploration, holds a special place within this series. Its significance lies not only in its timeless teachings but also in its timing. Paul wrote this letter just two decades after the crucifixion and resurrection of Jesus. It's a message still fresh in everyone's mind.

Our journey begins by unraveling Paul's profound messages to the church in Galatia, located in the southern part of modern-day Turkey.

These early Christians had backgrounds in paganism or views of Judaism as foreign. When Paul introduced them to the Gospel of Jesus Christ, he stripped away the trappings of religion and the entanglement of law, laying a foundation of pure, unadulterated grace.

However, challenges arose after Paul's departure. The Judaizers, Jewish believers in Christ who advocated merging the law with grace, began influencing the new converts, sowing confusion about the requirements of faith in Jesus. In response, Paul wrote a letter that left no room for ambiguity. He reinforced the unadulterated Gospel of grace, unburdened by the law. Galatians is a powerful testament to our freedom in Christ.

As we dive into this fascinating book, grab your Bible and prepare for an enriching journey through the pages of Galatians.

Part One

Unpacking The Gospel Of Grace

Chapter 1

Paul's Gospel of Grace

When we read the letters of Paul, we notice that he generally covers a specific area for a few verses before he transitions to another topic. We see this in Galatians chapter one verses one through five, and then again in verses six through ten.

Understanding Paul's Unshakable Authority

Galatians 1:1-5: *"Paul, an apostle (not from men nor through man, but through Jesus Christ and God the Father who raised Him from the dead), and all the brethren who are with me, To the churches of Galatia: Grace to you and peace from God the Father and our Lord Jesus Christ, who gave Himself for our sins, that He might deliver us from this present evil age, according to the will of our God and Father, to whom be glory forever and ever. Amen."*

In these verses, Paul qualifies himself as an apostle not by what he has done but because of what Jesus has done. If he spoke today in modern English, he might say, "I'm not coming to you with an ordination certificate or a seminary degree." Of course there is nothing wrong with those; I have both. But Paul makes it clear that it was not men who endorsed his authority or his message. This came as quite an insult to the Judaizers who were coming to these Galatians as long-standing, well-respected Jewish leaders whose teachings were founded on the traditions and approval of men. So from the very first line of his letter to the Galatians, Paul is establishing his authority as an apostle. He is letting them know that he isn't leaning on his religious background or degrees to qualify him to preach this Gospel. His message isn't rooted in men's wisdom, but as one sent directly from Jesus.

> Paul isn't the least bit intimidated. He's not a people pleaser, and he's not there to tickle their ears or preach an accepted popular doctrinal view. He's confident of the revelation he received and the message that he carries.

He preaches the uncompromised Gospel of grace with boldness without being arrogant or prideful. He's well-grounded in the message and he teaches it from a place of deep knowing. This kind of rich understanding takes time to sink in. Therefore, it becomes necessary for us to allow this truth to settle in, in order for us to minister grace from the same place of knowing that Paul did. If you allow the message to take root in you, it will easily flow from you to the people God brings across your path.

The True Meaning of 'Sin' Unveiled

> **Galatians 1:3-5:** *"Grace to you, and peace from the Father of our Lord Jesus Christ, who gave Himself for our sins that He might deliver us from this present evil age, according to the will of our God and Father, to whom be glory forever and ever. Amen."*

Paul lays out the objective truth of what Jesus fully accomplished — Jesus gave Himself for our sins and delivered us from the evils of this present age. That is the objective truth. It's a finished reality — He gave Himself for our sins. Paul then reveals something here that we often pass over when we read this passage. The Greek word for sin is the word *hamartia*, and it means to miss the mark. It's an archery term referring to the arrow missing the bullseye. He's not talking about sin as drinking, smoking, lying, or anything else the church typically labels as sin.

> Paul understood that the sin (hamartia) that Jesus came and gave Himself for, was us missing the mark of our authentic identity.

According to the Mirror Bible: "Sin is to live out of context with the blueprint of one's design; to behave out of tune with God's original harmony. *Hamartia* suggests anything that could possibly distract from the awareness of our likeness."

Every action or behavior we have labeled as sin arises from not knowing our authentic identity. **What we *do* is not who we are.** Our actions align with who we think we are. So, when you don't know your true identity, you begin to act like someone you aren't. Think of it like an actor playing a role. Our actions on the stage called life reflect the character we believe we are.

Jesus came to awaken us as sons. His life was a revelation of what a child of God's lifestyle should look like. When we understand that we're sons and daughters of God, made in His image and likeness, our behavior automatically changes. Religion focuses on trying to change our behavior when it should be teaching us how we've "missed the mark" through our weak and limited understanding of our authentic identity. As He is, so are we in this world. Our behavior is merely the outflow of our assumed identity.

> Religion teaches our identity from two starting points —
> the fall of Adam or the cross. Both begin with the faulty
> idea that we are separated from God.

If it begins in Adam, we automatically start with separation because religion teaches that sin separates mankind from God. If it starts at the cross, it also begins with separation because it's still about sin and our need to be reconciled to God. Colossians 1:21 says that we were alienated and separated *in our minds* by wicked works. Not knowing our authentic identity leads to evil works, which creates a mindset of separation from God. It's like losing our way in life.

Religion teaches that we are born inherently flawed, incomplete, depraved sinners. But when Paul lays down the foundation of our identity, he always takes us back before the cross and before Adam. In Ephesians 1:4, he says that God chose us in Christ before the foundation of the world. In choosing us in Christ before the foundation of the world, God set our identity, and from His perspective, we would be eternally without blame before Him in love.

While Paul informs the Galatian Christians that they have missed the mark and fallen from grace, he reassures them that this deviation is not attributable to their actions. The Judaizers, on the other hand, placed the entire focus on one's actions to attain righteousness before God, and they had been quite successful in persuading the Galatians that adherence to the Law was essential for salvation. The Apostle Paul is challenging the teachings of the Judaizers by prompting a shift in the Galatian's perspective, helping to renew their minds, and opening their eyes to the radical grace Gospel of *Jesus plus nothing*.

The last part of Galatians 1:4 says, "So that He might deliver us from the present evil age." Paul said something similar in Colossians 1:13, "He has delivered us from the power of darkness and conveyed us into the kingdom of the Son of His love." What is Paul doing? He is establishing in their minds that they, through

Christ, were placed into another kingdom apart from circumcision or works. Jesus alone did the placing, apart from any help from us. He gave Himself for our sins, and He delivered us from the evils of this present age, according to the will of God the Father. It's a finished reality. This is Paul's message straight out of the gate! He doesn't tiptoe into it, dance around it, or ease up on it. Instead, he hits it harder in verses 6-10.

Confronting Counterfeit Gospels

> **Galatians 1:6-10:** *"I marvel that you are turning away so soon from Him who called you in the grace of Christ, to a different gospel, which is not another; but there are some who trouble you and want to pervert the Gospel of Christ. But even if we, or an angel from heaven, preach any other gospel to you than what we have preached to you, let him be accursed. As we have said before, so now I say again, if anyone preaches any other gospel to you than what you have received, let him be accursed. For do I now persuade men or God? Or do I seek to please men? For if I still pleased men, I would not be a bondservant of Christ."*

In verse six, he said, "I marvel that you are turning away so soon from him that called you in the grace of the Lord, to a different gospel." When we don't progress in grace, we naturally tend to fall back into doing rather than just being. Paul called that another gospel, a perverted gospel. The word perversion means distortion. The Judaizers were distorting the Gospel of grace.

When something is distorted, it isn't seen clearly. But the Spirit of Truth is leading us out of distorted perceptions, and the message of grace apart from works is becoming clearer and sharper.

Paul goes on in verse eight and says, "But even if we or an angel from heaven, preach any other gospel to you than what we have preached, let him be accursed!" I love Paul's boldness. He's telling them that he has given them the authentic Gospel, and if anyone preaches something that strays from the Gospel of the finished work of Jesus, even slightly, they are disqualified! That's bold. Then he repeats this charge in verses 9 and 10, saying, "As we have said before, so now I say again, if anyone preaches any other gospel to you than what you have received, let him be accursed. For do I now persuade men, or God? Or do I seek to please men? For if I still pleased men, I would not be a bondservant of Christ."

Francois du Toit does an excellent job of translating these verses in the Mirror Bible and capturing the strength and boldness of what Paul is saying.

Galatians 1:9-10 from The Mirror says:

"Let me be blatant and clear about this: any gospel that does not emphasize the success of the cross is counterfeit and produces nothing but the curse. (In sharp contrast to the time when I needed letters of authority from the religious institutions of the

day endorsing my mission) *God is my complete persuasion. I answer to him alone, not anyone else. Christ employs me; I am addicted to his grace. Popular religious opinion will not influence me to compromise my message.* (What is the point of an impressive CV when your Maker is not even asking for it?)" **NOTE:** *The word "CV" used in the Mirror Bible notes, is short for the Latin "curriculum vitae," meaning "course of life"—which is a document much like a resume.*

Anything other than Paul's message of grace apart from works is a counterfeit gospel.

So, we must ask ourselves: has the church kept the post-resurrection grace message of the Apostle Paul? Or have we, like the Galatians, moved from it, and added works to the simplicity of grace? Does the Gospel we hear cause us to fix our eyes exclusively on Jesus? Hebrews 12:2 tells us to look to Jesus, the Author and the Finisher of our faith. If He's the Author and Finisher, then He's also everything in between. We must honestly ask ourselves: does the gospel I'm hearing cause my focus to be on Jesus plus nothing?

Distortion or perversion comes when doctrines, methodologies, formulas, laws, and rules are emphasized instead of what Christ has done for us, *as us*. In Philippians 3:14, Paul said, "I press toward the goal for the prize of the upward call of God in Christ Jesus." There's one prize, and it isn't found in denominations, churches, platform celebrities, doctrines, or formulas. It's only found in Christ. Does the gospel we hear today make us self-conscious or Christ-conscious? That's the question we must answer for ourselves.

Rediscovering the Simplicity of Grace

In the first ten verses of Galatians chapter one, Paul tells the churches in Galatia that they have lost sight of what Jesus has done for them and have shifted their attention towards how to make themselves acceptable. That same shift goes on today in many religious circles all over the world. The focus is not on Christ Jesus and what He has done, but on ourselves. We see our inability to keep all the laws, to dot every "i" and cross every "t" and it creates guilt and a sense of failure. That is not the Gospel; it's a counterfeit.

The authentic Gospel draws us to Christ. The perverted gospel will draw you to the good — but not to God. Radical transformation comes through *His* done; it never comes through *your* do. The proof of the authentic Gospel is in the fruit of people's lives. Paul's message transforms lives. Religion only alters appearances.

Paul's main concern for the Galatians was that they were moving away from this Gospel of grace. He encouraged them to come back to the simplicity of *Jesus plus nothing*. Paul's message was that Jesus has delivered us, saved us, and has caused us to no longer miss the mark. We have the stamp of authentic identity. We *are* the image and likeness of God.

Chapter 2

Paul's Journey to Radical Grace Begins

The Gospel message has always been about Jesus plus nothing. Religion, however, has added to it over the years, convincing us that we must labor and strive to become who we already are. As we move through this first chapter of Galatians, Paul shares his transformation from religion to revelation, which gives us greater insight into our own journey of grace.

Leaving Religion for Radical Grace

> **Galatians 1:11-14:** *"But I make known to you, brethren, that the gospel which was preached by me is not according to man. For I neither received it from man, nor was I taught it, but it came through the revelation of Jesus Christ. For you have heard of my former conduct in Judaism, how I persecuted the church of God beyond measure and tried to destroy it. And I*

> *advanced in Judaism beyond many of my contemporaries in my own nation, being more exceedingly zealous for the traditions of my fathers."*

Paul's origins were firmly grounded in Judaism. He received a comprehensive education, displaying a solid grasp of the Mosaic Law and the traditions of his forefathers. His religious fervor ran so deep that he genuinely believed he was carrying out God's divine purpose by capturing and killing Christians. However, in reality, he was a fanatical terrorist! He murdered people for embracing the message of grace apart from works, of the message of "Jesus plus nothing."

> **Verses 15-17:** *"But when it pleased God, who separated me from my mother's womb and called me through His grace, to reveal His Son in me, that I might preach Him among the Gentiles, I did not immediately confer with flesh and blood, nor did I go up to Jerusalem to those who were apostles before me; but I went to Arabia and returned again to Damascus."*

In Paul's own words, he offers a glimpse into his personal journey of grace, which carried him from the depths of his devotion to Judaism to the enlightening revelation of grace. Chosen by Jesus to deliver this message to the Gentiles, Paul narrates his shift from religious bondage to freedom.

> **Verses 18 through 24:** *"Then after three years I went up to Jerusalem to see Peter and remained with him fifteen days. But I saw none of the other apostles except James, the Lord's brother. (Now concerning the things which I write to you, indeed, before God, I do not lie). Afterward, I went into the regions of Syria and Cilicia. And I was unknown by face to the churches of Judea, which were in Christ. But they were hearing only, 'He who formerly persecuted us now preaches the faith which he once tried to destroy.' And they glorified God in me."*

In verse 11, Paul clarifies that the gospel he proclaimed did not originate from human sources. This understanding held immense importance for the Galatian church, as the Judaizers had entirely distorted the gospel with their man-made, religious interpretation of grace. Paul continues in verse 12, emphasizing that this gospel was not taught to him by any human being. It was a revelation directly received from Jesus Christ. In other words, he did not acquire it through formal education or conferences, nor did it come to him during a typical Sunday morning church service or by the laying on of hands to receive an impartation. It was a revelation directly from the Spirit of God and delivered by Jesus Himself.

When you receive spiritual revelation, it imparts a confidence that is neither haughty nor arrogant, for it is not a product of your cleverness and intellect. It aligns you with a different frequency, resonating with your inner man, allowing you to grasp it and make it your own. You no longer echo what you've been taught by religious tradition. Revelation turns you into a trumpet, capable of sounding a blast that resonates with others.

Paul asserts that because his revelation came from Jesus, it instilled an unwavering knowing, confidence, and boldness that strengthened him in the face of adversity.

In verse 13, he said, "For you heard of my former conduct in Judaism, how I persecuted the church of God beyond measure and tried to destroy it. And I advanced in Judaism beyond many of my contemporaries in my own nation, being more exceedingly zealous for the traditions of my father's." Paul's transparency in this passage is evident as he openly acknowledges that he formerly led a life saturated with fruitless religious rituals, misguided learning, and deluded priorities.

It's quite common for individuals to feel disheartened, and perhaps even experience anger or bitterness when they consider the consequences of false teachings by religious leaders who have lost their way. In Paul's case, he passionately believed that persecuting the church and taking the lives of believers was a way of pleasing God. Before his conversion, Paul said he was "exceedingly zealous" for his religious traditions. Religion will always try to snuff out Spirit revelation that doesn't agree with its man-made doctrines and rituals. In Colossians 2:6-7, Paul says, "As you therefore have received Christ Jesus the Lord, so walk in Him, rooted and built up in Him and established in the faith, as you have been taught, abounding in it with thanksgiving." Then he says in verse eight, "Beware lest anyone cheat you through philosophy and empty deceit, according to the tradition of men, according to the basic principles of the world, and not according to Christ."

Religion carries a zeal that seeks to stifle any enthusiasm or conviction regarding the revelation you've received. With its philosophies and traditions, it tries to negate this life of excitement that you have in Him.

> When you move from religion to revelation, there is usually a game-changing moment for you that changes everything. A pivotal shift occurs in you and sets you free from religious bondage.

Discovering the Christ Within

The Gentiles were pagan worshippers who thought they were excluded from the covenant of God and separated from Him. However, Paul receives a revelation that becomes the centerpiece of his message to the Gentiles, and it completely shakes up the religious world around him.

> **Galatians 1:15-16:** *"But when it pleased God, who separated me from my mother's womb and called me through His grace, to reveal His Son in me, that I might preach Him among the Gentiles... "*

God revealed His Son *in* Paul, and it radically changed how he saw himself. Christ was *in* him, even during his persecutions of the church and the murdering of Christians, although he was unaware of it at the time. Christ had *always* been in him. In verse 16, Paul doesn't say Christ was revealed to him. No, what he says is much more intimate and tangible than that. The message he preached was unprecedented, as he unveiled the mystery of the ages that the Father had disclosed within him — Christ is *in* the Gentiles. Christ is *in* all of humanity. Christ is *in* even non-Jewish pagan worshippers with no spiritual or religious background.

In verse 16, the word translated **in**, is the Greek word *en*, meaning a fixed position or in place. In other words, Paul was saying, "It pleased God to reveal Christ, His Son, *who had a fixed place within me.*" That's the clear Gospel, eliminating any idea of separation, the distinction between the privileged and the excluded, the "us" and the "them," or the insiders and outsiders of God's covenant. There are no outsiders in God's covenant! It dispels the religious concept of requiring people to pray a specific prayer to be saved, insinuating that without it, Jesus cannot dwell in them. In actuality, the truth is that Christ lives *in* all — regardless of who we are.

For many years, I held the belief that God had to personally introduce Christ *to* Paul, just as I assumed it was necessary for each of us. I presumed that, like us, Paul (as Saul) was separated from God and required the Holy Spirit to introduce him to Jesus before He could live in him. However, in reality God revealed the Son *in* him so that Paul could preach the mystery that was hidden for generations, which is Christ *in* the Gentiles, *even* in the midst of their unbelief in God. This message remains as pertinent today as it was when Paul preached it.

We need to shout this message from the rooftops to those in correctional facilities, prisons, halfway houses, and in every church throughout America and around the world.

People need to grasp the truth that they have never been separated from God because Christ dwells in them; this was Paul's message of grace; this is the Gospel.

In Colossians 1:26-27, Paul said, "There is a mystery which has been hidden for ages and from generations, but it's now being revealed to the saints. To them, God will make known what are the riches of the glory of this mystery among the Gentiles: which is Christ in you, the hope of glory... ." I don't know where we got this idea that we had to ask Jesus to come live in our hearts and dwell inside us. This verse in Colossians is a powerful proof text indicating an awakening to what is already a reality. **Being in union with Christ made humanity a brand-new**

creation. We're not refurbished versions of our old selves; we are not remakes. Through our union with Christ, humanity became a distinctive and unprecedented species that the world has never seen before; we are a new creation. All of humanity has a changed DNA.

Is that what Peter was getting at in 2 Peter 1:4, when he said, "by which have been given to us exceedingly great and precious promises, that through these you may be partakers of the divine nature." We didn't receive just a portion of His divine nature; we received the entirety of it. His divine nature became a permanent part of us, taking up residence within us, when we were united in resurrection with Jesus. We were co-crucified, co-buried, co-resurrected, co-ascended, and co-seated with Christ. This co-event in Christ ushered in the era of a new creation.

The Gospel message is that Christ is *in* all.

When Jesus went to the cross, all humanity went with Him — in Him. The old Adam died. That entire ancient race of humanity died. There is only the new creation *in* the Last Adam, Who is Christ. Romans 5:19 says, "For as by one man's disobedience many were made sinners." As a result of Adam's disobedience, many were made sinners. In other words, mankind was duped and no longer knew their identity as sons of God, made in His image and likeness.

Consequently, their actions reflected a distorted identity. The rest of verse 19 says, "...also by one Man's obedience many will be made righteous." Righteousness took up a fixed position within humanity. This righteousness is embodied in a Man, Jesus, who is the Christ. We were made righteous through the death, burial, and resurrection of humanity and Christ *as one*.

Maturing in Revelation During Paul's Desert Journey

> **Galatians 1:16-17:** *"I did not immediately confer with flesh and blood, nor did I go up to Jerusalem to those who were apostles before me; but I went to Arabia, and returned again to Damascus."*

Paul went into the desert to let this revelation of hyper-grace settle within him. He had to spend time in solitude, away from the influence of religious voices, allowing the Spirit of Truth to continue working in him. Why didn't he rush out and share this incredible revelation with everyone? Why didn't approach the apostles or go to Jerusalem to announce the groundbreaking news that Christ dwells *in* all men? The initial stage of revelation can be somewhat unclear. Paul needed time to let this message sink deep into his being, becoming an unwavering and unshakeable truth within him. Had he shared it prematurely, others might have influenced or even talked him out of it. He needed to safeguard the purity of the revelation by allowing it to mature and solidify within himself.

Verses 17b-24: *"...but I went to Arabia, and returned again to Damascus. Then after three years, I went up to Jerusalem to see Peter and remained with him fifteen days. But I saw none of the other apostles except James, the Lord's brother. (Now concerning the things which I write to you, indeed, before God, I do not lie.) Afterward I went into the regions of Syria and Cilicia. And I was unknown by face to the churches of Judea which were in Christ. But they were hearing only, 'He who formerly persecuted us now preaches the faith which he once tried to destroy.' And they glorified God in me."*

In these verses, Paul offers a glimpse of his life after receiving the monumental revelation of Christ in the Gentiles from the Holy Spirit. He returned home and cautiously began sharing his testimony, traveling to various places and connecting with believers. Paul didn't opt for grand auditoriums, flyers, or extensive advertising to attract crowds. He took a simple and straightforward approach sharing what Christ had shown him and the profound transformation it had brought to his own life.

Then in verse 24 it states that they begin to glorify the God they saw in him. When God releases you to share revelation, go easy with it; go to those He leads you to share with. Holy Spirit will confirm it in them, producing fruit in their lives, and in turn they will glorify God in you.

In verses 13-16, Paul said, "For you have heard of my former conduct in Judaism, how I persecuted the church of God beyond measure and tried to destroy it. And I advanced in Judaism beyond many of my contemporaries in my own nation, being more exceedingly zealous for the traditions of my fathers. But when it pleased God, who separated me from my mother's womb and called me through His grace, to reveal His Son in me, that I might preach Him among the Gentiles."

Paul is traveling this road going from religion to revelation when he is hit with a "but," that turns his world upside down. It was as if a switch was flipped within Paul when he comprehended that Christ dwelled *in* him. The light of this understanding instantly transformed his entire life. The powerful thing about light is that it unfailingly dispels darkness. Darkness cannot endure in the presence of light. Light and love eliminate all fear of torment.

The Christ *in* you illuminates what He finished for you and *as you*, driving out all of your doing.

Embracing Four Profound Shifts in Grace

In an instant, you realize that all of your works are like filthy rags. This awakening occurs as Christ within you opens your eyes and reshapes your perspective. Transitioning from religion to revelation, four profound transformations begin to arise within you

1. The confidence that the same grace which brought us into a full relationship with the Christ in us will be the grace that keeps us.

We don't go in and out of grace by attempting to modify our behavior through adherence to man-made doctrines. Grace not only keeps us but also effortlessly changes us from within. Ephesians 4:7 affirms this by stating, "But to each one of us, grace was given, according to the measure of Christ's gift." Additionally, in Ephesians 2:7 Paul indicates that it will take ages for God to show us the exceeding riches of His grace in His kindness toward us in Christ Jesus. God's grace is inexhaustible, and our confidence surges when we recognize that He brought us in by grace and intends to sustain us by grace. He doesn't expect us to maintain grace by our actions.

In Ephesians 4:6, the statement, "There's one God and Father of all who is above all, through all, and in all," carries a profound revelation on the journey from religion to revelation. It signifies that the Father of all takes full responsibility for us. He didn't seek our permission or acceptance; He simply graced us. His grace is strong enough to uphold us, independent of our efforts.

2. We realize that we have already been given all things.

We don't need to wait for God's presence to show up or for the Holy Spirit to descend upon us. We don't have to engage in fasting or prayer as a means of convincing God. Christ in us instills the confidence and knowing that we already possess all things. This truth is echoed in Romans 8:32, which states , "He who did not spare His own Son, but delivered Him up for us all, how shall He not with Him also freely give us all things?" That understanding has revolutionized my approach to prayer. I can't recall the last time I petitioned for something in prayer. Now, I understand that with Christ, I have freely been given all things. If God deemed it important enough to provide us with Christ, it's unquestionable that He also freely gave us everything else.

Consider Jesus Himself; He never prayed for His needs to be met, be it finances, a place to live, or a donkey to ride. He knew that He possessed all things. John 16:15 affirms, "All things that the Father has are Mine." Jesus lived from the Source of all things, and out of that Source, He accessed the supply in any form required.

That's what Paul's driving at with the message of Christ in you. When Jesus took up residence within you, He brought with Him everything that belonged to Him. Paul stated in Galatians 2:20 that he was crucified with Christ, and he no longer lives, but Christ lives within him. Paul lived in the full reality of this inward life.

3. A righteous consciousness comes from the revelation of Christ in us.

With that revelation, all sense of sin consciousness goes. The righteous consciousness of Jesus and the sin consciousness cultivated by religious practices cannot coexist in the same space. As soon as the light of understanding dawns, the darkness dissipates. When the righteous consciousness takes root, the burdens of works-righteousness are expelled. Grace Himself displaces anything that fosters a sense of sin consciousness. Effortless change occurs as you acknowledge and recognize the presence of Christ within you. There's no longer a need for striving as He brings about the transformation from the inside out.

4. Christ restores the Living Word to a position over the written word.

Most of us have come from church backgrounds that took the Bible as the absolute, unfailing source for all aspects of life. However, the true guide should be the Spirit of Truth within us, leading and directing us. The Bible is not meant to be our moral compass dictating how to live or what actions to take or avoid; that's the realm of the Tree of the Knowledge of Good and Evil. Rather than serving as a rulebook, the Bible should point us toward an encounter with Jesus and the revelation of Christ in us, who is the Tree of Life.

> The Bible isn't a life guide; the Spirit of Truth dwelling within us is the Guide of Life, and He is present because Christ is in us.

Allow the Spirit of Truth to lead you. Allow Him to establish the Christ in you as the foundation for every good thing you experience from this point onward. Learn to resist the pressure of those who would impose rules and restrictions, attempting to curtail your liberty and freedom in Christ. Also, resist the mental inclinations that strive to establish standards you must meet. These aspects are not inherent in the life you share with Christ, who dwells in you. Embrace your freedom and liberty, recognizing that you are called to live with full awareness of the continual unveiling of the Christ within you.

Chapter 3

The Transformation of Grace

Embracing the path of grace is undeniably a journey of liberation, though it may present its share of challenges. Moving from the confines of religious doctrine to the enlightenment of revelation can be disorienting, particularly at the beginning, giving rise to moments of doubt and uncertainty. It's not uncommon to question whether you've truly grasped the message. However, the encouraging truth is that if you persist, there comes a pivotal moment when you cross a threshold, and gradually, the message becomes an integral part of your belief system, just as it did for Paul. It becomes your personal Gospel.

Suddenly, you gain confidence in your convictions, find yourself adept at articulating them clearly, and engage in profound conversations with others. At this juncture, there's no looking back. The allure of returning to the shackles of religious dogma diminishes, and the world around you bursts into vibrant life. This fresh perspective revitalizes your mind and transforms your existence, allowing you to perceive yourself, God, and your surroundings through an entirely new lens.

Paul's 14-Year Transformation: A Time of Preparation

> **Galatians 2:1:** *"Then after fourteen years I went up again to Jerusalem with Barnabas, and also took Titus with me."*

Following his life-altering encounter with Jesus, Paul spent three years in the Arabian desert. Then over the next 14 years, he began his ministry here and there as he matured in this message of grace. Eventually, Paul presented this radical message to the prominent Jerusalem church leaders: Peter, James, and John. But what was Paul doing for those 14 years of his life? Those years served as a hiatus or sabbatical, a period of refining his beliefs and theology by shedding layers of accumulated religious thinking. In his own words, he was a Pharisee among Pharisees, deeply immersed in legalism. However, his encounter with Grace Himself turned his world upside down. It took time to uproot those deeply ingrained religious mindsets and fully grasp the revelation of God's scandalous grace. It was a time of preparation.

Grace was taking root in his life during this period. The Gospel was becoming *his* Gospel!

The journey of truly owning the truth takes time. From the moment you catch a glimpse of the truth of grace to the point where you are as comfortable with it as Paul was, calling it *your* Gospel, there's a journey of growth. Paul's message was revolutionary, entirely unlike anything people had heard before. It wasn't a doctrine taught anywhere else; it was direct communication from Jesus to Paul, meant to be shared with the world.

During those 14 years, he didn't have books or YouTube videos for reference. He didn't have grace-oriented friends to discuss it with over lunch. It was just him and Jesus as this message took root in him. Many of the truths he shared in Galatians, Ephesians, Philippians, and Colossians likely emerged during those 14 years of preparation. These concepts shifted from being mere theories to daily experiences. Over that time, he lived out this message, matured in grace, and began to manifest the very grace he would later teach. Maturity developed as he surrendered to the process. Before moving forward though he would meet with the leaders in Jerusalem.

A Bold Political Move: Paul's Meeting with Jerusalem Leaders

> **Galatians 2:2:** *"And I went up by revelation, and communicated to them that gospel which I preach among the Gentiles, but privately to those who were of reputation, lest by any means I might run, or had run, in vain."*

Upon the ascension of Jesus, Peter, James, and John emerged as the leaders of the first-century church in Jerusalem. Paul recognized their significance and believed that a personal meeting with them regarding his message was crucial. It was a smart political move, as he understood that without their direct understanding and support, his message might be dismissed. Given their substantial influence over the people, Paul couldn't afford his preaching efforts to be in vain. Additionally, when he visited Peter, James, and John, he brought Titus, a Gentile.

> **Verse 3-4:** *"Yet not even Titus who was with me, being a Greek, was compelled to be circumcised. And this occurred because of false brethren secretly brought in (who came in by stealth to spy out our liberty which we have in Christ Jesus, that they might bring us into bondage)."*

However, some secretly infiltrated this gathering with ulterior motives. These individuals aimed to bring Paul, Barnabas, and Titus back into religious bondage. Their agenda was to subject them to the Law's influence, as the early believers, primarily Jewish, were grappling with a mix of law and grace. Regrettably, there is still a mixture of law and grace today in the Western Evangelical churches. We must learn how to recognize it so, like Paul, we won't be swayed by it.

> **Verses 5-6:** (Paul said) *"... to whom we did not yield*

> *submission even for an hour, that the truth of the gospel might continue with you. But from those who seemed to be something — whatever they were, it makes no difference to me; God shows personal favoritism to no man — for those who seemed to be something added nothing to me."*

I love Paul's unwavering boldness. He wasn't swayed by the religious positions people held or impressed by their status. He never deviated from his core message. The opposition he faced often came from legalistic teachers who sought to intertwine works with grace. These Judaizers believed that even though Jesus had done much for us, we still needed to do something for Him. For them, the Gospel remained transactional — a quid pro quo. They believed that if they did something for God, He would reciprocate. In contrast, Paul stood firm, emphasizing that it was all about grace, with nothing else required, and all about Jesus, with nothing more needed. This was a message he refused to compromise.

Clash of Titans: Paul, James, and John

As we read the writings of Paul, James, and John, we might notice a seeming clash between Paul's emphasis on grace alone and the inclusion of works in the teachings of James and John. It's important to remember that James and John addressed audiences in a different context than our modern-day Christianity.

> **Verses 7-9:** *"But on the contrary, when they saw that the gospel for the uncircumcised had been committed to me, as the gospel for the circumcised was to Peter (for He who worked effectively in Peter for the apostleship to the circumcised also worked effectively in me toward the Gentiles), and when James, Cephas, and John, who seemed to be pillars, perceived the grace that had been given to me, they gave me and Barnabas the right hand of fellowship, that we should go to the Gentiles and they to the circumcised."*

Peter, James, and John approved Paul's message and allowed him to focus on preaching to the Gentiles while they continued their ministry among the Jews. At that time, they might have believed that including the Gentiles was acceptable, thinking it might not have a lasting impact, so they might as well let Paul do his thing.

So Peter, James, and John went to the Jews with a mixture of law and grace. And Paul went to the Gentiles with the pure Gospel of grace — of grace apart from any works of the Law. Peter, James, and John were ministering to a transitional generation, teaching about Jesus post-cross, trying to transition those who had been under the Law. It was a bridge for those Jews coming out of religion and into grace. When Paul wrote this letter to the Galatians, only about 15-20 years had passed since the crucifixion and resurrection of Jesus. The memory of the Law of Moses and its customs and rules was still vivid in everyone's minds. People were continuing to visit the Temple daily for prayers and animal sacrifices.

But after the cross, it's a whole different ball game. Life had changed. Humanity has changed. All has been made new. Even today, the most challenging group to bring into the full Gospel of grace are often those deeply entrenched in denominational rules, with their many do's and don'ts, much like the Old Covenant Jews who were bound by their traditions.

For instance, consider 1 John 1:9, a verse commonly referenced in churches today. It states, "If we confess our sins, He's faithful and just to forgive us our sins and to cleanse us from all unrighteousness." What was the Jewish understanding of forgiveness of sins? In the pre-cross era under the Law, sins were forgiven through animal sacrifices in the Temple. John is teaching that this old sacrificial system of the Law has been abolished. If they need to clear their conscience, they should *confess* their sins, knowing that God is faithful and just to forgive them.

While it represents a shift from the old system to the new covenant of grace, John still introduces an act — the confession of sin—to seek forgiveness. However, it's important to recognize that his audience consisted of Jews who lived before the cross. John's inclusion of this action is to steer them away from the accustomed practice of animal sacrifices and established religious traditions. He is easing them into a new way of thinking, assuring them that they need only confess their sins to God if they feel compelled to take action. In doing so, they can trust in His faithfulness and justice to forgive without the need for an animal sacrifice.

We observe a similar approach in James 2:14. James asks, "What does it profit, my brethren, if someone says he has faith but does not have works? Can faith save him?" Because our eyes have been opened to grace apart from works, our immediate response would be, "Certainly!" However, James says in verse 20, "But do you want to know, O foolish man, that faith without works is dead?" Then, in verse 24, he asserts, "You see then that a man is justified by works, and not by faith only." And finally, in verse 26, he states, "For as the body without the spirit is dead, so faith without works is dead also."

But Paul taught a different message than James and John. When Paul came to the Galatians, he told them to stop mixing law and grace and to stop adding works to grace. He reminded them that they were never under the law and that what the Judaizers proposed had nothing to do with them. So, then, what exactly was Paul's teaching on grace and works?

> **Romans 3:28:** *"Therefore, we conclude that a man is justified by faith, apart from the deeds of the law."*

Paul says justification is by faith apart from works, while James says faith without works is dead. Hmmm! Those are two vastly different messages. In many Western Evangelical churches, you'll hear pastors read from James, prompting action, and then swiftly quote Paul's message from Romans, emphasizing justification by faith alone. So, which one is correct? Are we justified by faith apart from works, as Paul teaches? Or are there works we must add to faith, as James suggests? The risk of misunderstanding arises when you don't consider the context and audience.

When you read Peter, James, and John, you must understand the audience, context, and historical period they were writing. Paul is the New Covenant theologian, and back in verse five of chapter two, he said that he didn't yield to the mixture of law and grace *for even a moment*. Why? He goes on to say in verse 5, "that the truth of the Gospel might continue with you." He specifically warned the Galatians against the influence of the bewitching Judaizers.

I recommend reading my book, *Unhook the Book*, as it well help you understand how to rightly divide the Old and New Covenants.

The Influence of Modern-Day Judaizers: Calvinists & Arminians

In contemporary times, certain religious groups significantly influence our understanding of grace and liberty. These modern-day Judaizers can be identified as adherents of two theological perspectives: **Calvinism and Arminianism. Their perspectives have distorted the Gospel of grace.**

Calvinism originated in the 16th century under the leadership of John Calvin. Calvinists hold the belief in the total depravity of humanity, which means that all individuals are born in a state of depravity, sin, and separation from God. According to their theology, God is Supreme and All-powerful, choosing some for salvation while rejecting others. This doctrine leads to the belief that God's choices are arbitrary, and some are predestined for salvation while others are predestined for condemnation, or eternal conscious torment. This view portrays a God who is highly selective in His favor, a perspective not rooted in a correct understanding of the nature of God as Love.

On the other hand, **Arminianism** presents a different viewpoint. It suggests that God loves all individuals equally but has chosen not to exercise His sovereignty over their salvation. According to Arminian theology, the decision for salvation rests in the hands of humanity. This perspective can lead to the wrong understanding that human will is the ultimate determining factor in salvation. Believers in this theological tradition often emphasize the necessity of living a sinless life in order to maintain salvation and find favor with God.

Understanding the influence of these modern-day Judaizers, who mix aspects of law and grace, is essential. Both groups tend to reinterpret scripture to align with their respective doctrines. It is crucial to recognize when their teachings incorporate "works" or actions that one must perform. In light of this influence, it is essential to adopt an approach like that of the Apostle Paul — steadfastly refusing to yield to mixed messages and unwavering in the commitment to grace.

The Unveiled Gospel of Grace: All Included

The essence of the revelation of grace is that it transcends these faulty theological positions. Holy Spirit is bringing together the sovereignty found in Calvinism and the love found in Arminianism and combining them into a unified Gospel of Inclusion. That's the Gospel that Paul preached. This Gospel declares that God is sovereign and All-powerful, and His will is done no matter how many eons it takes because He loves all men equally. He is the God and Father of all. There's one Man who was predestined: Jesus. He was the Lamb slain from the foundation of the world. For all men! And not only *for* all men but *as* all men. He loves all sons equally.

The Gospel of Grace declares:

- He chose us and placed all men in the first begotten Son before time began. (EPHESIANS 1:4)
- One died for all therefore, all died (2 CORINTHIANS 5:14)
- Humanity was crucified with Christ; it was a co-crucifixion (GALATIANS 2:20)
- Humanity rose with Him (ROMANS 6:4-8)
- Humanity ascended and was seated with Christ in heavenly places. (EPHESIANS 2:6)

The gospel of inclusion takes the best of Calvinism and Arminianism and merges it. Both had a part of it right, but they couldn't quite wrap their heads around it. They saw through a glass darkly. So what does Paul do? He cleans the glass and shows us clearly who God is. 1 Timothy 4:9 says, "This is a faithful saying and worthy of all acceptance." What did Paul say was the faithful saying worthy of everyone's acceptance? Verse 10: "For to this end we both labor and suffer reproach, because we trust in the living God, who is the Savior of all men, especially of those who believe." Notice Paul doesn't say it's exclusively for those who believe. He says, *especially* to those who believe. Is there value in believing? Absolutely. Believing is an effortless response to revelation.

Paul's belief in Jesus was a direct result of encountering Him on the Damascus Road. When Jesus reveals Himself to an individual, the experience is so intense and deep that it effortlessly leads to belief. This belief enables one to experience and enjoy all that Jesus has finished for us and *as us*. But your believing or not believing does not affect the reality that He is the Savior of all men. He remains our Savior, irrespective of an individual's belief.

However, our belief holds significance and offers benefits because it brings us to a conscious awareness of the abundant spiritual inheritance we already possess in Christ.

Chapter 4

Grace Unleashed: Overcoming Hypocrisy and Religion

The Galatians had embraced the Gospel of grace and were enjoying their freedom. Paul wasn't about to let anyone undo that and put them under bondage again — not even Peter! In Galatians two, Paul describes an encounter with Peter that highlights the hypocrisy of trying to embrace both law and grace. In verses 11-15, he exposes Peter's double mindedness, showing that law strengthens sin. Those who condemn sin most loudly often talk about law the most. James 1:14 says, "Each person is tempted when drawn away and enticed by their own lust." What is James conveying? **When law is at work in your life, it entices you to sin.**

For example, someone makes a New Year's resolution not to eat desserts or sweets for a month. What does this do? It sets up a law in their life. Then what happens? They fail and eat sugar before the month ends. Why? The pull of whatever is forbidden becomes irresistible, and they do what they vowed not to. As Paul taught in Romans 7:5, "When we were controlled by our sinful nature, sinful passions aroused by the law worked in our bodies to bear fruit for death." Sinful passions awake in our lives because of the law.

The beauty of grace is that it transcends the limitations of the law. While some worry that too much emphasis on grace could lead to sinful behavior, it's vital to understand that grace doesn't condone sin. Instead, it empowers people to resist it, offering a liberation not found in rigid rule-following. In my experience, individuals entangled in sin often fixate on a strict moral code, struggling more than those who embrace grace. It's a joy to guide people from this restrictive mindset to a freer way of living. The law's allure is strong, especially for those with deeply ingrained beliefs. Yet, transformative change comes effortlessly through allowing the Holy Spirit to work within, not through behavior modification. As exemplified in Galatians 2, Paul calls out Peter's hypocrisy to show how the law can create double standards.

WHEN GRACE CONFRONTS LAW: EXPOSING PETER'S HYPOCRISY

> **Verse 11 states,** *"Now when Peter had come to Antioch, I withstood him to his face because he was to be blamed."*

Peter was one of the leaders of the first-century Jerusalem church, yet here's Paul confronting him for hypocrisy. If anybody should have gotten a hold of the message of grace, it should have been Peter. God gave him a tremendous of the inclusion of all humanity in Acts chapter 10, but he could not grasp it to the full extent that Paul did.

> **Acts 10:9-16:** *"The next day, as they went on their journey and drew near the city, Peter went up on the housetop to pray, about the sixth hour. Then he became very hungry and wanted to eat; but while they made ready, he fell into a trance and saw heaven opened and an object like a great sheet bound at the four corners, descending to him and let down to the earth. In it were all kinds of four-footed animals of the earth, wild beasts, creeping things, and birds of the air. And a voice came to him, 'Rise, Peter; kill and eat.' But Peter said, 'Not so, Lord! For I have never eaten anything common or unclean.' And a voice spoke to him again the second time, 'What God has cleansed you must not call common.' This was done three times. And the object was taken up into heaven again."*

The vision Peter had in Acts Chapter 10 marked an amazing turning point for him, making it crystal clear that in God's eyes, no one is unclean; instead, we are all seen as clean, righteous, justified, and holy. Such an encounter should be life-changing. Verse 15 states, "What God has cleansed you must not call common."This divine message shattered the religious exclusiveness rooted in Peter's Jewish background. It conveyed no distinctions between "ins and outs" or "us and them." Yet somehow Peter didn't fully embrace God's grace after that immense revelation. Because here in Galatians, we see him slipping back into a religious mindset that categorized people as Jewish or Gentile, clean and unclean.

Galatians 2:11 states when Peter visited Antioch, Paul confronted him face to face. Why?

> **Verses 12-13:** *"For before certain men came from James, he would eat with the Gentiles; but when they came, he withdrew and separated himself, fearing those who were of the circumcision. And the rest of the Jews also played the hypocrite with him, so that even Barnabas was carried away with their hypocrisy."*

In Antioch, before the other Jews arrived from Jerusalem, Peter ate with the Gentiles — breaking the Mosaic Law while eating non-kosher food and thoroughly enjoying the freedom of grace! However, as soon as the other Jews arrived, Peter felt the religious pressure to fall back into the dos and don'ts of the law, to separate himself from those who were not like him — from those considered unclean by the religious leaders. Don't we tend to do the same thing today? We feel pressure to conform to religious traditions, so we don our robes of righteousness on Sunday but live a very different life Monday through Saturday. That's what religion does and what Peter demonstrated.

So, in verses 14-21, Paul lays out the grace Gospel applying to both Jews and Gentiles.

> **Verses 14-21:** *"But when I saw that they were not straightforward about the truth of the gospel, I said to Peter before them all, "If you, being a Jew, live in the manner of Gentiles and not as the Jews, why do you compel Gentiles to live as Jews? We who are Jews by nature, and not sinners of the Gentiles, knowing that a man is not justified by the works of the law but by faith in Jesus Christ, even we have believed in Christ Jesus, that we might be justified by faith in Christ and not by the works of the law; for by the works of the law no flesh shall be justified. "But if, while we seek to be justified by Christ, we ourselves also are found sinners, is Christ therefore a minister of sin? Certainly not! For if I build again those things which I destroyed, I make myself a transgressor. For I through the law died to the law that I might live to God. I have been crucified with Christ; it is no longer I who live, but Christ lives in me; and the life which I now live in the flesh I live by faith in the Son of God, who loved me and gave Himself for me. I do not set aside the grace of God; for if righteousness comes through the law, then Christ died in vain."*

Paul beautifully contrasts the law's futility with Christ's sufficiency for all. Verse 15, which reads, "We who are Jews by nature, and not sinners of the Gentiles," demands clarification. He's saying

Jews and Gentiles all sin the same way — *missing the mark of authentic identity*. In other words, when identity is misunderstood, Jews and Gentiles act the same. **The core issue lies in a misunderstanding of identity**. Jews believed they were exceptional if they adhered to the Law, thinking this would earn them acceptance from God. However, Paul shatters this misconception by asserting that both Jews and Gentiles sin in the same manner; they all fall short of recognizing their true identity as beings created in the image and likeness of God.

Righteousness Through Christ's Faith

The first part of Galatians 2:16 says, "Knowing that a man is not justified by the works of the law…" Yet James, in chapter two, verse 24 of his letter, says that a man is justified by works and not by faith only. James is writing to a Jewish audience, not to Gentiles. (See James 1:1) He is not living out of the depth of grace that Paul is teaching. So Paul straightens it out when he says, "Knowing that a man is not justified by the works of law, but by the faith of Jesus Christ."(KJV)

If you have a New King James or some other translation, it says, "knowing that a man is not justified by the works of the law but by faith in Jesus Christ." The word "in" is the wrong preposition used in this verse. If you look at the original text, it says, "We are saved by the faith *of* Jesus Christ." The translator put the word "in" there, most likely because of personal prejudice, thinking that you must have faith "in" Jesus to be justified.

But that's not what Paul said. King James translation got it right: "Knowing that a man is not justified by the works of the law, but by the faith *of* Jesus Christ, even we have believed in Jesus Christ, that we might be justified by the faith *of* Christ, and not by the works of the law: for by the works of the law shall no flesh be justified."

The Jews, in particular, should have grasped this concept, as they were well aware of the impossibility of perfectly adhering to the Law. Yet, even though they themselves, including the Pharisees, struggled to keep it, they persistently imposed it on others. Religion still does this today. Denominations teach rules, laws, and regulations that even their own leaders find challenging to uphold, yet they burden others with these expectations. **Justification comes through Jesus' faith, not ours. It's all His doing.** He is the Author and Finisher.

> **Verses 17 to 19:** *"But if, while we seek to be justified by Christ, we ourselves also are found sinners, is Christ therefore a minister of sin? Certainly not! For if I build again those things which I destroyed, I make myself a transgressor. For I through the law died to the law that I might live to God."*

In verse 19, Paul says that they died to the Law. And verse 18 says that if they return to the Law, they put themselves under the law of sin and death. Paul was strong about not being under the law of sin and death.

Freedom from Condemnation: No Judgment in Christ

In Romans 8:1, he says, "There is therefore now no condemnation to those who are in Christ Jesus." Who is in Christ Jesus? Everyone! Ephesians 1:4 says God put us in Christ before the foundation of the world. No one has to live under condemnation — it's self-imposed, not from God.

> There's a difference between the conviction of the Holy Spirit and condemnation from self or others.

Condemnation will always move you away from a sense of God's presence. Conviction by the Holy Spirit always leads us to an awareness of the presence of God. When the Holy Spirit convicts us, He wraps His arms around us and lets us know how loved, accepted, and included we are. He draws us back into the love of God. His conviction reassures us that we are in Christ free from any condemnation.

Paul is telling us not to get under condemnation. In Romans 8, he says, "There is therefore now no condemnation to those who are in Christ Jesus, who do not walk according to the flesh, but according to the Spirit." Walking after the law of sin and death puts us under condemnation because it's a mixed message. No one was able to keep the Law. In Christ, there is only grace — law and grace cannot coexist together. The way you stay free from condemnation is to walk in an understanding of the law of the Spirit of life that is in Christ Jesus.

In Galatians 2:21, he said, "I don't set aside the grace of God, for if righteousness comes through the law, then Christ died in vain." Paul says Christ defines us; we were co-crucified with Him two thousand years ago. We were in Him every step of the way, from the crucifixion to the ascension. We died our death with Christ. A man was appointed to die once, and that appointment was met when we were co-crucified with Christ. Death has no more dominion over us, just like it has no more dominion over Jesus. (SEE ROMANS 6:9)

Paul says in verse 21 that if we could attain righteousness by keeping the law, then Jesus didn't need to come; we could do it on our own. By thinking we achieve it through our own doing, we set aside what He has done for us and *as us;* we set aside grace. What does it mean to set aside grace? Essentially, we are saying that His death and grace are irrelevant, and we can do it all alone.

> Everywhere he went, Paul taught the truth regarding the co-inclusion of man with Christ, as the all-sufficient One, and the power of grace, invalidating any law of performance for justification.

In these first two chapters, Paul prominently emphasizes the grace of God. He is sharing the Father's love that He has lavishly and freely poured out equally on all humanity. Pouring it out even when we had nothing to bring to the table and nothing to offer that would warrant it. Salvation is a free gift. Paul soundly rejects the idea of a transactional gospel, where God's grace depends on our accepting, loving, tithing to, or worshiping Him in exchange for salvation. Instead, Paul stresses that God's grace does not rely on human effort or work. It is an unmerited gift given purely because of God's love and mercy, without Him expecting anything in return. It's a message of grace that stands in contrast to a quid pro quo or transactional approach to salvation.

The more you sink into the relationship that Paul talks about here, the more it elevates your frequency. It raises your vibration, and you begin seeing what Paul taught in his letters. Why? Because what Paul was writing in these letters is now on the same frequency as your understanding, and suddenly you are blown away by the sheer magnitude of God's excessive and outrageous grace, and it's way more liberating than any radical hyper-grace believer could ever fathom. You begin to see verses from your Bible that you never saw before, showing you just how good God really is.

Grace vs. Religion: Unveiling the Liberating Gospel

Allow me to walk you through some verses you may have never heard taught correctly in church...

- **John 12:47:** "If anyone hears my words and does not believe, I do not judge him. For I did not come to judge the world but to save the world."

Many of us used to believe that if we heard His word and didn't act upon it, we would be subject to judgment. However, this interpretation doesn't align with John 12:47. Thanks to His scandalous, unreasonable, over-the-top, and unexplainable grace, He declared that He would not judge anyone! Why does He refrain from judgment? Because He didn't come to judge the world but to save it. **So, the critical question to ask yourself is this: Did He accomplish it? Was He entirely successful in saving the world?**

- **Second Timothy 2:13:** "If we are faithless, He remains faithful."

Many of us may have once believed that God's obligation to us would cease if our faith waned. Why? We thought our faith drove His faithfulness. However, Paul reassured Timothy that even when our faith falters, God remains steadfast because His faithfulness is an inherent part of His character, and He cannot deny Himself.

- **John 5:22:** "For the Father judges, no one."

I grew up with the idea that one day, I'd stand before the Father, and He would open His book on judgment day, recounting all my misdeeds. I even imagined the possibility of these transgressions displayed on a massive screen for all to see — every failure laid bare, leaving me in shame and without a defense. But Jesus said the Father judges no one, having committed all judgment to the Son. And what does the Son do? Three chapters later, in John 8:15, Jesus states, "You judge according to the flesh; I judge, no one." So, where does judgment originate? From ourselves, others, culture, thoughts, and teachings — not the Father or the Son. Neither the Father nor the Son passes judgment on our actions.

> Jesus's only judgment is that you are righteous, justified, holy, a son, brother, and joint heir with Him. That is His judgment of you.

This one-way Love says, "Come to me as you are. Give up doing and striving. Lay it down. Rest in Me, and as you do, I will work in you an effortless change." That's how good He is. He lives in you. His love is unconditional. Do you understand the depth of the word unconditional? It means there are no stipulations, add-ons, or asterisks to His love for you. He fully lives in you and has held nothing back. Colossians 2:9 says, "In Jesus dwells all the fullness of the Godhead dwells bodily." All of the fullness of the Godhead lives in Jesus, and He held none of it back from you! Verse 10 says, "And you are complete in Him." So if you're complete in the One in whom all the fullness of the Godhead dwells, the same fullness in Jesus dwells in you.

Paul goes even deeper with it in verse 13: He said, "And you, being dead in your trespasses and the uncircumcision of your flesh, He has made alive together with Him, having forgiven you all trespasses," What did you bring to the table? Nothing good! The only thing you brought to the table was your deadness in your trespasses and sins. Your contribution was a messed-up mind. Yet in sovereign grace, God made you alive in Christ.

This gratuitous, over-the-top grace came when we had zero to offer. It has always been and will always be about Him and His eternal work, not us.

Religion's Veil Over Grace

Religion often seeks to reintroduce us to a scenario similar to what the Judaizers attempted to impose on the Galatians. It endeavors to draw us into the idea that we must contribute to what Jesus accomplished entirely on His own, without needing our assistance or effort. The Judaizers' approach was to persuade the Galatians to earn this salvation through obedience, discipline, fasting, and strict adherence to laws, among other things. Religion says, "After all He's done, can't you do something for Him? Hold up your end!" Whether ancient Judaizers or modern fundamentalists, religion plays on feelings of obligation and showing love, gratitude, and appreciation through our actions.

In Galatians 2, Paul moves them from "we must do for Jesus" religiosity to awakening to what Jesus did for all humanity — waking us up to God's unconditional acceptance, choice, and love. Like Paul, John got it: "We love because He first loved us." (1 John 4:19) Paul teaches that everything we do is in response to what Jesus has already done. It's in response to His initiative. We don't need to pray the magic prayer, confess our sins, or demonstrate faith to elicit a response from God.

Believing or having faith doesn't make anything happen; it can only awaken you to what has already happened. Your confession doesn't make it happen, either. The Greek word for **confession** is *homologeo*, meaning "to agree with." Confession is simply agreeing with what God has already demonstrated and given to you. Grace elicits an effortless response to His revelation of who He is. The more He unveils who He is, the more our understanding of Him deepens, and our belief grows stronger. To each of us, grace has been given according to the measure of the gift of Christ. Grace is a big gift!

Paul said in 2 Corinthians 4:3, "If our gospel is veiled, it is veiled to those that are perishing." Perishing doesn't mean they're headed to hell. It means that they are experiencing a disconnect from *the* Source of life. Paul is saying that if the Gospel of freedom, liberty, and crazy, over-the-top grace is hidden, and we're not getting it, our understanding is darkened. In verse four, he says, "Whose minds the god of this age has blinded, who do not believe, lest the light of the gospel of the glory of Christ, who is the image of God, should shine on them." When that light shines, the veil is lifted, and we can truly see.

The "god of this age" comprises anything occupying our minds and time — whatever drains energy and diverts us from our path. It is what blocks clear vision and action toward our goals. **Religion tries blocking the light and freedom of the Gospel with laws and rules.** It does so because it doesn't want to relinquish control over individuals. Paul's message to the Galatians is the contrast between the liberating grace of the gospel and the constraints imposed by religious rules and traditions.

The Unchanging Truth of God's Goodness: Love That Never Fails

Religion doesn't want the Gospel viewed through Paul's lens, fearful of losing influence. When the radiant light of the Gospel shines within you, you no longer rely on religion's formulas and steps to attain righteousness, holiness, and favor in God's eyes. God indeed demands that we be righteous and holy, but His diagnosis was that all had fallen short of hitting the mark, and His solution was Jesus is our righteousness, *as us*. Paul said in 1 Corinthians 1:30, "But of Him, you are in Christ Jesus, who became for us wisdom from God—and righteousness and sanctification and redemption." Religion encourages striving to attain wisdom, righteousness, sanctification, and redemption, but Paul's message is that these qualities are already ours through Jesus. Second Corinthians 5:21 says that He made Him who knew no sin to be sin for us, that we might be made righteous with His righteousness.

Paul was passionately preaching the good news given to him directly by revelation from Jesus. He understood that when the light of this message dawns on individuals, it will transform our world. His message to the Galatians of this Gospel of grace was not *too good to be true*. It's the truest truth of the universe — one-directional, unconditional Love will fulfill God's plan for every person born, regardless of how long it may take.

Love never fails, not once for anyone. That is the demonstration of authentic grace. Even when religion tries to choke out the goodness of God, it does not alter the truth of God's goodness.

Chapter 5

Grace in Action

In Galatians 3, Paul tackles the law-grace conflict head-on by addressing the Galatians personally, speaking to them as if engaged in a one-on-one conversation, expressing intense emotion of amazement at their foolishness. This chapter holds great relevance today, especially in the Western Evangelical churches. Regrettably, many individuals still find themselves trapped in the very predicament Paul addresses — a mixture of law and grace. Often, we fail to recognize the subtle manner in which the law influences our thoughts and actions. A "balanced" grace with a few added requirements seems normal. But Paul confronts the dangerous mixture infecting the Galatians' understanding of grace.

Law and Grace on a Collision Course: A Lethal Combination

The law today for modern Christianity is not about the Ten Commandments or the 613 laws of Moses. Instead, the term "law" encompasses all the numerous "dos" and "don'ts" that religion deems necessary for salvation or obedience. As Paul addresses the Galatian believers, his primary concern is getting entangled in a mixed message after they've received the pure Gospel of grace. This kind of mixed message generates feelings of guilt, condemnation, and a sense of separation from God due to our perceived failures and shortcomings.

I can relate to this from my own experience. There was a period in my life when I believed that if I didn't start my day with an hour of prayer, I would feel guilty, thinking that God might not be as favorable toward me as He would if I had spent that hour in prayer. Now, there's nothing inherently wrong with dedicating an hour to prayer in the morning, but it becomes problematic when it evolves into a standard or a requirement to maintain a position of favor and goodness in the eyes of God.

In Colossians 1:21, Paul states that our previous sense of alienation and enmity with God, stemming from our wrong actions, *was a mental perception.* We were never separated from God because of wrong actions. It was all in our minds. Paul continues by saying, "...yet now He has reconciled in the body of His flesh through death, to present you holy, and blameless, and above reproach in His sight."

> It was all His doing — through the body of His flesh, through His death — He reconciled us.

> Our holiness, blamelessness, and being above reproach are all because of Him!

Begin to see yourself how God sees you as holy, blameless, and above reproach in His eyes. There is nothing we need to do to earn that. It is not a progressive work in our life. We are fully holy, fully blameless, and fully above reproach. It was all His doing. Many people come into that freedom, but then they somehow slip back into a "grace" that demands self-effort. That's not grace. **There is no self-effort in grace.** Instead, it's a *falling from grace*.

I used to think that falling from grace was to fall into sin. But that's not what Paul taught. In Galatians 5:4, he says, "You have become estranged from Christ, you who attempt to be justified by law, you have fallen from grace." According to Paul, falling from grace is not about falling into sin but falling back under the bondage of the law after discovering the freedom of the Gospel.

> Mixing law and grace is the absolute Ishmael of the gospel — taking a promise from God that only He can fulfill and trying to accomplish it through our efforts.

That's the situation Paul addresses in this third chapter of Galatians. He's writing to people who entered the freedom of grace, but religious leaders have talked them out of that liberty back into restraints, standards, laws, rules, and regulations.

In Galatians 3:1, Paul takes a very personal approach to his message. He doesn't merely address the entire church corporately but brings it down to an individual level. He admonishes them by saying, "O foolish Galatians! Who has bewitched you that you should not obey the truth, before whose eyes Jesus Christ was clearly portrayed among you as crucified?" He's telling them that they have lost all common sense. Paul initially preached the good news about the crucified Jesus and the completed work of the cross to the Gentiles, and they were beginning to live in the freedom and grace that this message offered. However, he goes on to explain that someone came and cast a spell on them, deceiving them into believing that what Jesus accomplished wasn't sufficient and that additional actions from them were necessary.

> **Verses 2-5:** *"This only I want to learn from you: Did you receive the Spirit by the works of the law, or by the hearing of faith? Are you so foolish? Having begun in the Spirit, are you now being made perfect by the flesh? Have you suffered so many things in vain — if indeed it was in vain? Therefore He who supplies the Spirit to you and works miracles among you, does He do it by the works of the law, or by the hearing of faith?"*

It's all by grace. Why do we think we can add to it through our actions? Can you see how easy it is to fall into that pit? When we do that, we are headed back to Egypt, back to the place of bondage, having fallen from grace by putting ourselves back under the law. Grace and law cannot co-exist.

Paul asks in verse five, "Therefore He who supplies the Spirit to you and works miracles among you, does He do it by the works of the law, or by the hearing of faith?" If we can't get it through good works or merit it by our actions, why do we believe we can perfect and maintain it through our efforts? What comes by liberty and grace can't be perfected by our efforts.

Abraham's Faith: A Blueprint for Trusting God

In Galatians chapter three, verses six through nine, Paul uses Abraham as an example of how this works. The righteousness of Abraham didn't come because he was good; it came because he believed God alone was able to do what He had promised.

> **Galatians 3:6-9:** *"Just as Abraham believed God, and it was accounted to him for righteousness. Therefore, know that only those who are of faith are sons of Abraham. And the Scripture, foreseeing that God would justify the Gentiles by faith, preached the gospel to Abraham beforehand, saying, 'In you all the nations shall be blessed.' So then those who are of faith are blessed with believing Abraham.'"*

Abraham's faith was not faith in his faith. He was unable to fulfill what God had promised. It wasn't about him having enough faith to "get" what God had promised. Thinking back, how much time did you spend building up your faith to receive what God had promised you? Incorrectly believing things like *maybe I didn't get healed because I lacked faith*. And so you blamed all your "unfulfilled" promises on your lack of faith, personal shortcomings, or something else you weren't doing right in your life, thinking if you could fix it and build up your faith, all would be well. No. Paul is saying that the promise that comes from God is for us to believe that God alone can do what He said He could do — apart from our ability. That's the example he gives us of Abraham, who trusted solely in God's ability to do what He promised to do.

For God to do what He promised, Abraham had to get out of the way. And so do we. To walk into the full manifestation as sons of God, we have got to get out of the way. Ishmael was a result of Abraham trying to produce something God had promised. How many Ishmaels have we created because we felt like God promised something, but we didn't see the manifestation right away, so we tried to do it through our efforts?

When Abraham was 75, God promised to give him a son despite his wife Sarah being well past childbearing years. God's promise seemed physically impossible, and after at least a decade of waiting, Abraham took matters into his own hands. Abraham tried to produce what God had promised through his efforts, resulting in an Ishmael.

In Romans chapter four, Paul tells a bit more about the situation with Abraham, and it directly relates to what we're talking about in Galatians chapter three — trying to perfect in the flesh what God promised and gave us in the Spirit. Romans 4:4-5: "Now to him who works, the wages are not counted as grace but as debt. But to him who does not work but believes on Him who justifies the ungodly, his faith is accounted for righteousness." We're not getting it by grace if we try to work for it.

> **Romans 4:17-22:** *"(as it is written, 'I have made you a father of many nations') in the presence of Him whom he believed—God, who gives life to the dead and calls those things which do not exist as though they did; who, contrary to hope, in hope believed, so that he became the father of many nations, according to what was spoken, 'So shall your descendants be.' And not being weak in faith, he did not consider his own body, already dead (since he was about a hundred years old), and the deadness of Sarah's womb. He did not waver at the promise of God through unbelief, but was strengthened in faith, giving glory to God, and being fully convinced that what He had promised He was also able to perform. And therefore 'it was accounted to him for righteousness.'"*

Much like he did with Abraham, Paul instructs us not to boast in our abilities. Living in the Spirit requires us to release control and trust God, and therein lies the essence of freedom. Let go of the burden that you must produce results in your life. If God has made a promise to you, trust that He will fulfill it. He accomplishes what seems impossible to us. In verse 17, he said, "Abraham, I made you the father of many nations, in the presence of Him whom he believed God has given life to the dead, and calls things that do not exist as though they did exist." Reviving the dead is not something we can do in our ability. When God does something, He doesn't need your help. When God promises something, He can deliver what He promises. It's not our job to bring about the fulfillment of God's promises.

Paul emphasizes the need for the supernatural to bring reality into existence. That's where grace enters in. Grace alone makes it possible. In Romans 4:18, Paul says, "Who, against all hope, believed in hope." All we have is hope. Hope is a focused expectation that God will do what He's said. Your trust and your hope bring you into the blessing. It's about leaning into His promises, expecting them, but refraining from trying to manifest them to fruition through your own efforts. God does require our assistance.

All God needs from us is to believe He can do it, and believing is a simple, effortless response to what He reveals.

Let's shift our attention to another example — a pair of sisters who are vivid illustrations of law and grace.

Mary & Martha: The Choice of Rest or Striving

In Luke 10, we encounter two sisters: one who lives in the unforced rhythms of grace and the other who strives to gain Jesus' favor through her actions and self-imposed standards. This narrative paints a beautiful contrast between the concepts of law and grace.

> **Luke 10:38-42:** *"Now it happened as they went that He entered a certain village, and a certain woman named Martha welcomed Him into her house. And she had a sister called Mary, who also sat at Jesus' feet and heard His word. But Martha was distracted with much serving, and she approached Him and said, 'Lord, do You not care that my sister has left me to serve alone? Therefore tell her to help me.' And Jesus answered and said to her, 'Martha, Martha, you are worried and troubled about many things. But one thing is needed, and Mary has chosen that good part, which will not be taken away from her.'"*

When Jesus enters their home, He discovers Martha diligently working to serve Him. She's bustling in the kitchen, preparing food and getting everything ready based on her assumptions of what Jesus might need. In contrast, her sister Mary is at Jesus' feet, simply savoring His presence without concern for work. Martha soon grows irritated at Mary's failure to serve Jesus. Even now, in church culture, the non-striving Marys frustrate the task-focused Marthas. This frustration often stems from the perception that we must actively serving to please Jesus and earn His favor.

Mary enjoys resting in Jesus' presence, while anxious Martha tries hard to prepare unrequested food to please Him. Martha's irritation with Mary eventually leads to frustration with Jesus because He doesn't seem to expect the same actions from Mary that she believes are necessary. Martha's perceived obligations were entirely self-imposed. All Jesus desired from both sisters was for them to rest in and enjoy His presence.

> God doesn't want us to labor incessantly to earn His favor, nor does He require us to prove our love by our actions.

Martha's life serves as a vivid illustration of what happens when we mix law with grace. Jesus entered her home out of love, not merit, yet Martha busied herself trying to earn His love. Law will never let us lean back into the arms of Grace and relax. It's important to remove any hint of legalism and religious bondage from our lives. Some of the best-known grace teachers in the world today still carry strains of law. We must learn how to spot it and say no. We need to know how to rightly divide the covenants.

Colossians 2:13-14 says, "And you, being dead in your trespasses and the uncircumcision of your flesh, He has made alive together with Him, having forgiven you all trespasses, having wiped out the handwriting of requirements that was against us, which was contrary to us. And He has taken it out of the way, having nailed it to the cross." Jesus took away all of the laws, *even the self-imposed ones we would place on ourselves*. He took *every* ordinance contrary to us and nailed it to the cross. The law-based system of the Old Covenant died two thousand years ago. **We are not under the law but under grace. They cannot co-exist.**

Embracing the Completed Work: It's a Done Deal!

That's what Paul drives home in the first nine verses of Galatians chapter three. He is letting them know that the Father doesn't make transactions with us. The Gospel is not if you pray the prayer, have faith, repent, pay your tithes, or _____ *(fill in the blank)*, then He'll bless you. No, we find the Gospel in 2 Corinthians 1:20, which says, "ALL the promises of God in Him are Yes, and in Him Amen, to the glory of God through us." (EMPHASIS MINE) Every promise in Him is yes and amen.

Any promise you find in the Bible, or better yet, one that He speaks in you, is yes and amen. **It's not an "if you do, then He will do it" transaction. His promises are a done deal.** When He makes a promise to you, it is yours. He has already given you everything that pertains to life and godliness. Just like the father told the elder brother, who was striving and slaving to earn acceptance, "ALL that I have is yours."

Romans 8:32 says, *"He who did not spare His own Son, but delivered Him up for us all, how shall He not with Him also freely give us all things?"*

It's all been finished for us and as us and freely given to all to enjoy. He took striving for it out of the equation. **He's given you ALL things, apart from your praying, claiming, confessing, begging, etc.** All that He has is already yours. Enjoy it!

Chapter 6

Breaking Free With Grace

In Galatians Chapter 3, verse 10, it says, "For as many as are of the works of the law are under the curse; for it is written, 'Cursed is everyone who does not continue in all things which are written in the book of the law, to do them.'" The real problem with the law is that it's a continual cycle of frustration and failure. You'll never be satisfied with how much you're doing, and you'll keep adding to it. Galatians 3:10 (Mirror Bible) says, "In clear contrast to faith, the law is the authority of the curse. As it is written, 'Everyone who fails to perform the detailed requirements of the law, even in the least, is condemned.'" Failure to fulfill the law or any self-imposed requirements you've placed on yourself will always result in condemnation.

> You can't become any more acceptable to God than you already are. Your acceptance is a done deal.

Escaping the Heavy Burden of the Law

Works of the law consist of anything you must do to receive what God has already said is yours. There are no additional requirements necessary to obtain what Jesus finished for you and *as you*. But that's what the Judaizers were telling the churches in Galatia. They were coming through and proclaiming that it wasn't enough to rest in what Jesus had done; they needed to be circumcised and keep the Law. That sounds similar to what we hear in most churches today: Jesus finished His part, but it's ineffective until we do ours. **That's not a covenant; that's a contract.**

Jesus' cry from the cross, "It is finished," extends far beyond mere effectiveness. There is nothing we can do to put the finishing touches on what Jesus has already done.

The Church's Shift: Departing from a Christ-Centered Gospel

That's what stopped the church cold in its tracks — they ceased being Christocentric. Jesus was no longer at the center. The church introduced various man-made stipulations they considered essential to earn God's approval, much like what the Judaizers did with the Galatian Christians. They asserted that hearing the Gospel and accepting Jesus was good, but grace alone wasn't sufficient; to attain true righteousness, they must adhere to specific requirements from the Law. Religion does the same thing today, teaching that grace isn't enough and giving us man-made doctrines and conditions for salvation and righteousness. It's why the church is so weak today. It keeps us running in circles, striving to do what Jesus already did.

> **Verses 10-13:** *"For as many as are of the works of the law are under the curse; for it is written, 'Cursed is everyone who does not continue in all things which are written in the book of the law, to do them.' But that no one is justified by the law in the sight of God is evident, for 'the just shall live by faith.' Yet the law is not of faith, but 'the man who does them shall live by them.' 'Christ has redeemed us from the curse of the law, having become a curse for us (for it is written, 'Cursed is everyone who hangs on a tree,')'"*

Verse 10 says that the Law produces the curse when not entirely obeyed. Paul is conveying that if the Galatians heed the Judaizers' teachings, the continuous flow of *zoe* — the Divine life which emanates from grace — suddenly stops. How does this apply to us today? Simple: if we heed the teachings of the Western Evangelical Church, which often emphasizes strict adherence to laws and rules, we miss out on experiencing the abundant life of God. Allowing the rules and regulations of the evangelical church to permeate our lives can obstruct this life-giving flow. If we don't keep growing in grace, allowing God's grace to penetrate deeper within us, we may unintentionally regress into a self-imposed system of laws; this is what's referred to as backsliding, which is not a descent into sin, but falling from grace to living under the law.

> When you detect that familiar performance-driven mentality resurfacing, you need to stop it in its tracks right then and there.

SICKNESS, DEATH, AND POVERTY: THE CURSE OF THE LAW

The curse or penalty of the Law (disobeying the Law) is threefold:

- Sickness
- Death
- Poverty

Deuteronomy 28:15 says, "But it shall come to pass if you do not obey the voice of the LORD your God, to observe carefully all His commandments and His statutes which I command you today, that all these curses will come upon you and overtake you." It lists approximately 1,518 curses, all falling into three significant categories: sickness, death, and poverty. Galatians 3:13 says that Jesus redeemed us from the curse. But what does **redeem** mean exactly? It means to save from loss.

Therefore, when Jesus redeemed us, He rescued us from the impending loss resulting from sickness, death, and poverty, effectively eliminating it. He eliminated it. Christ has saved us from the loss of the curse of the law by becoming the curse for us — **He became sickness, death, and poverty *as us*.**

Matthew 8:17 says, "… that it might be fulfilled which was spoken by Isaiah the prophet, saying: 'He Himself took our infirmities And bore our sicknesses.'" He took our infirmities and bore our sicknesses.

He took what belonged to us through the curse of the Law — infirmities, and sicknesses — and absorbed it.

Second Corinthians 5:14 says, "For the love of Christ compels us, because we judge thus: that if One died for all, then all died;" In addition to our infirmities and sicknesses, He took our death — if One died for all, then all died. Given that we have already undergone death through Christ, why do we still experience it today? Remember, *we are as He is in this present world*. In John 10:18, Jesus declared with authority, "No man takes My life. I lay it down, and I pick it up again."

Paul grasped this truth. The exact number of times Paul died is uncertain, but it's reasonable to assume it occurred on numerous occasions, quite possibly at least six or seven times. Acts 14:19 says he was stoned, dragged outside the city gates, and left for dead. Stoning was a death sentence. The final stone they used was a giant stone to crush someone's head. But what happened when the religious crowd stoned Paul? He got up and walked into town. There's just no way around it. Paul died and came back to life.

Not only did Jesus take on our illnesses and mortality, but 2 Corinthians 8:9 also reveals that He assumed our poverty. This verse states, "For you know the grace of our Lord Jesus Christ, that though He was rich, yet for your sakes, He became poor, that you through His poverty might become rich." Despite His inherent wealth, He willingly became poverty so that you could have His riches as your own.

Jesus absorbed all humanity into Himself and all the curses resulting from our inability to keep the Law. Jesus came and fulfilled the Law for us and *as us*. Then, through His death on the cross, He absorbed all of it into Himself, completely dissolving it. **In doing so, He redeemed and rescued all humanity from sickness, death, and poverty.**

> The undeniable truth is that humanity has been redeemed from the curse. So why do we still experience death, poverty, and sickness?

The root of the issue lies in our failure to perceive ourselves as free from these afflictions. If you can't envision your freedom, how can you ever experience it? You can't possess what you're unable to see. Proverbs says, "As a man thinketh in his heart, so is he." It's time we get honest about how we see ourselves. The problem isn't external; it's internal, and religion has fed into this dilemma. Some of the most broke, sick, depressed people identify as Christians. There is something wrong with that. They aren't recognizing their freedom from the curse of loss, sickness, poverty, and death despite Jesus having redeemed and rescued us.

> The core issue lies in their struggle to believe they were rescued.

Will an immediate transformation occur if we adjust our beliefs? Probably not, but that's where steadfastness comes in. The critical question is how we respond when our circumstances contradict what God has revealed as true about us. Will we yield to these circumstances, or will we tenaciously hold onto the revelation of grace in our hearts? Does this imply we should passively wait and do nothing? No, because He will guide our actions and direct our steps in what we need to do in alleviating sickness, poverty, or death.

Our Divine Inheritance: The Blessing of Abraham

Galatians 2:14: *"That the blessing of Abraham might*

come upon the Gentiles in Christ Jesus, that we might receive the promise of the Spirit through faith."

God made a covenant with Abraham, promising he would experience blessing in all his endeavors. He assured Abraham that every place he set foot upon would be his and God would be his constant Guide and Protector. In verse 14, Paul conveys to the Galatian church that Abraham's blessings were theirs in Christ, not by adhering to the Law. The same is true for us; we have inherited the blessing of Abraham. It's not something we earn, but we do merit it. What does this mean? Our co-crucifixion and co-resurrection in Christ made us worthy of receiving this inheritance. We aren't mere beggars, pilgrims, or strangers in a foreign land, just passing through until we make it to heaven someday. God blessed Abraham to be a blessing to all the nations. That includes us—we are part of the "all nations."

This blessing is abundant enough to encompass every individual in the world.

There is no shortage of supply; the problem lies in the distribution. Recently, I came across a startling fact: every year in America, we waste 133 billion pounds of food, which amounts to nearly one-third of the available supply. There is an overabundance that could easily feed everyone. God has blessed our fields, harvests, and everything we put our hands on. The problem doesn't stem from God's provision but from our mishandling of His provision. Philippians 4:19 says, "My God shall supply all of your needs according to His riches in glory."

Has He done that? Absolutely. So where's the problem? We haven't followed the example of Joseph; we've neglected the distribution and failed to be good stewards of what God has placed in our hands.

We have been blessed in every area of life — that's Kingdom living. I love that Paul gets so brutally honest in this third chapter of Galatians. He calls them foolish Galatians! They were thoughtless, without understanding, not reasoning out the matter to the end. They were being dragged out of grace and into law because they weren't allowing Godly wisdom to inform their views and beliefs. When you start poring over what Jesus has finished for you and as you, there is absolutely no room left for you to embrace any law or standard that requires you to earn anything from God.

> Over and over, Paul reiterates how futile it is to try and do anything to obtain what grace has freely bestowed and what Jesus has already done.

When we begin to sense feelings of inadequacy, tempted to fall back into performance mode, we must remind ourselves that grace is not merited by behavior. We must allow the Spirit of Grace to show us areas that have been sacred cows in our belief systems and let grace tip those over so we can experience freedom in *every* area of our lives.

Chapter 7

The Transformative Power of Words

Before we move on from Part I to transition into Part II of the book, I'd like to dedicate this chapter to examining four pivotal words that Paul uses in his epistles and give you clear insight into Paul's perspective of these words. The wisest man who ever lived said in Proverbs 18:21, "Death and life are in the power of the tongue, and those who love it will eat the fruit of it."

> Our words possess the remarkable power to produce either life or death. They are important and greatly impact our perception of the world around us.

Science has shown us how our words can significantly affect our physical bodies. For example, our bodies react physically to both positive and negative words. Positive words can help strengthen and improve a person's well-being, while negative words can do physical and emotional harm. Therefore, how we define the words we speak becomes extremely important. Unconsciously, our brain takes words and converts our perceived definitions into pictures that ultimately create the reality we experience and live in.

So, if we have an inaccurate definition, it builds a defective perception, creating a flawed reality. For instance, Western religion has entirely redefined the word church, forming the mental picture of a building for us. But that's not what the word church initially meant. When Jesus said, "I will build my church," the word He used was *ecclesia*, which means "called out ones." Jesus is talking about people, not a building. In its original definition, the word church always referred to people. However, because religion has changed the meaning of the word, our perception of "church" is based upon a faulty definition.

Reclaiming the Language of Grace

In his epistles, Paul uses four words — *confession, believing, faith, and receiving* — that must be correctly defined if we are to understand and grasp the full meaning of the Gospel Paul was preaching. Just like with *ecclesia*, religion has redefined the meaning of these four words from what Paul originally meant. **Religion always starts from a premise of separation from God and what we must do to bridge the gap.**

It's the 'if and then' transactional gospel of Western Christianity — if you do something for God, then He will do something for you.

Paul never started with separation. He always began with union and the inclusion of all men because of the finished work of the Cross. With Paul, there's no quid pro quo.

Religion has cemented the meanings of these four words around the idea that we have entered into a contract with God. In other words, it teaches us that we must do our part by confessing, believing, having faith, and receiving, *and then* God will respond favorably to us. However, Paul never used them in the context of work or performance on our part.

Let's examine these four words from Paul's perspective…

Confession: Agreeing With God

The church has redefined confession as coming to God and acknowledging our sins so He can forgive us. The word **confess** in Greek is *homologeo*, meaning "to agree with or to say the same thing." Paul's use of confession (*homologeo*) means to align ourselves with God's perspective on a matter and agree with Him about it. In essence, when we confess our sins, we articulate God's perspective on sin, concurring with His established view. However, we must know God's stance on sin to do this effectively.

> **Colossians 2:13:** *"And you, being dead in your trespasses and the uncircumcision of your flesh, He has made alive together with Him, having forgiven you all trespasses."*

He has forgiven us all our trespasses. Therefore, when approaching Him regarding our sins, we should align ourselves with His perspective and echo what He says about sin. In light of this, my confession becomes: *"Father, I acknowledge that You have already forgiven me for all my sins and trespasses."*

> **Hebrews 8:12:** *"For I will be merciful to their unrighteousness, and their sins and their lawless deeds I will remember no more."*
>
> **Hebrews 10:17** is similar. It says, *"Their sins and their lawless deeds I will remember no more."*

These verses are clear: God doesn't even remember our sins anymore. So, how can we ask God to forgive us for a sin He doesn't even remember? Therefore, our confession needs to agree with Him, saying what He says: *"Father, I know You don't remember my sins. Therefore, there is no need to confess a list of things I've done wrong."*

But Don, what about 1 John 1:9? It states that we must confess our sins so He can forgive us.

Yes, 1 John 1:9, says: "If we confess our sins..." But remember, confess *(homologeo)* simply means saying and agreeing with what God says about our sins. We just learned in Colossians 2:13, Hebrews 8:12, and Hebrews 10:17 what God says about sin. God said He has already forgiven and forgotten all of them. He no longer remembers them. So, if we genuinely confess and agree with God — saying what He says about our sins, we know He's faithful and just to forgive us and cleanse us from all unrighteousness — we will see and understand the finished work regarding sin.

Instead of making our confession a work or something that we must do to be forgiven, we need to begin to use the words of our mouths to confess and come into agreement with God, saying, "Father, I messed up on this one, but I know that You don't even remember it. It's already forgiven. It's not part of who I am. It's not me."

Understand that what you do is not who you are. Who you are is forgiven, justified, sanctified, redeemed, and made in the image and likeness of God. 1 John 2:12 says, "I write to you, little children, because your sins are forgiven you for His name's sake." Why haven't we given 1 John 2:12 as much attention as we did 1

John 1:9? Religion pushes the idea that we are separated from God because of sin and has mistakenly used 1 John 1:9 to redefine the meaning of confession, thus necessitating our requirement of confession for our sins to be forgiven. In contrast, Paul teaches us that confession or *homologeo* is agreeing with God and saying the same thing He says. If we are to agree with Him, let's agree with 1 John 2:12, which tells us that He has already forgiven our sins for His namesake.

> The same approach we applied to "confession" can be used for "salvation" — aligning with God and echoing His words.

The verses most frequently cited in connection to salvation are found in Romans chapter 10. It says in Romans 10:9-10, "that if you confess with your mouth the Lord Jesus and believe in your heart that God has raised Him from the dead, you will be saved. For with the heart one believes unto righteousness, and with the mouth confession is made unto salvation."

So, what does the Father say about salvation because we want to align our words and agree with what He already says? In Luke 19:10, we have Jesus' confession, "I came to seek and to save that which was lost." So, our confession is realizing that Jesus came to seek and save what was lost, and He was 100% successful. Our confession (*homologeo*) doesn't grant us salvation; it simply reflects our agreement with what Jesus proclaimed about our salvation. He declared that He came to seek and save that which was lost, and clearly, He didn't require our assistance in seeking or saving the lost. Our confession serves as a realization of this truth.

Which leads us to the second term, "believing," also found in Romans 10:9-10.

Belief: The Effortless Response to Divine Revelation

Believing is simply an effortless response to revelation. I used to think that I had to take action to make something a reality. One day, I finally realized that we are unable make ourselves believe anything. It's the Holy Spirit's job to convince us of what is true. The Spirit of Truth was sent to bring us light and revelation that we can respond to. And the beauty of it is when He brings the light and revelation, we believe, sometimes even before we consciously recognize we're believing.

Isn't that what transpired with Saul, who became Paul on the Damascus Road? When Jesus appeared to him, shedding light on the truth, Paul dropped his religious façade, his years of training, his persecution against the church, and he simply just believed. He uttered, "Lord, what do you want me to do?"

> God knows our hearts. He knows how to persuade each of us with the truth, and once we see it, we will effortlessly respond to it.

Religion often instructs us that it's our responsibility to generate belief rather than entrusting the Holy Spirit to persuade us. Many churches emphasize that if we want God to do something for us, like heal us or save us from hell, *we* must take the first step to believe. However, the crux is that we cannot honestly believe in God as our Healer until the Holy Spirit personally unveils that truth within our hearts. When this revelation occurs, we believe and effortlessly respond, and its impact manifests in our lives.

Considering what we've uncovered about Paul's comprehension of confession, let's revisit Romans 10:9-10 and paraphrase it using the definition that believing is a natural response to revelation, and confession involves aligning with God and saying what He says.

> **Romans 10:9-10:** *"For if you will confess (say the same thing and agree with God) the Lord Jesus Christ, believe (respond to the revelation on the inside) in your heart that God raised Him from the dead, you will be saved."*

Religion has transformed these two verses into a laborious endeavor by redefining the terms "believing" and "confession." It has placed the responsibility on individuals to muster faith, believe, and confess to attain salvation. One must jump through all the hoops, dot all the i's, and cross all the t's before God will extend salvation. This interpretation doesn't align with Paul's original intention in these verses.

Paul teaches that we agree and say who Jesus is based on the revelation and light we have seen. My perception of Jesus now far surpasses what it was five or ten years ago. As I effortlessly responded to the Holy Spirit's unveiling of truth within, life flowed into me that I hadn't ever experienced before.

Let me present the Keathley translation: "If you agree and say who Jesus is, based on what has been revealed to you, then wholeness will begin to work in your life. From the depths of your heart, your spirit man, you grasp the revelation, and your words harmonize with that revelation."

We must stop echoing verses in the manner religion has redefined them and, instead, grasp their meaning through Paul's understanding of what Jesus finished for us and *as us*.

Faith: Trusting in God's Unlimited Power

This word, faith, has caused so much stress and condemnation in the body of Christ. When God's promises fail to materialize in our lives, or when healing doesn't occur, and things don't unfold as anticipated, we tend to shoulder the blame, convinced our faith was inadequate. However, it was never meant to revolve around our faith. **Faith is fundamentally a belief in God's capability, not a reliance on our own.** It was never intended for us to place our faith in *our* faith. Faith is trust; it's unwavering dependence on Him.

Faith alleviates the burden from us and squarely rests it on Him. It hinges on the Father's capacity to fulfill what He has declared, nothing more. It's about having complete confidence in Him.

Romans 10:17 says, "Faith comes by hearing and hearing by the Word of God." This verse was never intended for us to compile a set of scriptures from the Bible to bolster our faith. It's worth noting that the Bible doesn't refer to itself as the Word of God. There is only one infallible Word of God, and it's not a written text; it's the person of Jesus — the Word Incarnate. Jesus *is* the flawless Word of God. The Word of God you hear is the word that God speaks directly to you, which carries within it the faith required to trust what He communicates.

We've often regarded faith as something we must cultivate within ourselves to achieve various outcomes, such as healing, financial well-being, salvation, justification, and more. We erroneously believed that our self-generated faith was the mechanism by which these things transpired in our lives. We assumed we had to "by faith" appropriate what Jesus had already provided.

Romans 4:19-21 recounts the narrative of Abraham and serves as an excellent illustration of faith. It says, "And not being weak in faith, he did not consider his own body, already dead (since he was about a hundred years old), and the deadness of Sarah's womb. He did not waver at the promise of God through unbelief, but was strengthened in faith, giving glory to God, and being fully convinced that what He had promised He was also able to perform."

That is the essence of faith. All of the burden was lifted from Abraham to perform or bring the promise to pass. When God imparts something to you, His spoken word carries within it the power to have confidence in Him to bring it to pass. Regrettably, we have sometimes reversed this concept and wrongly believed that when God speaks to us, it automatically becomes our responsibility to achieve it or make it happen through our faith. I've experienced disappointment countless times due to what I perceived as my "lack of faith."

> In reality, faith is nothing more than unwavering trust in the capacity of the One who made the promise and complete assurance that He is fully capable of carrying it out.

Receiving: Embracing Our Divine Inheritance

Receiving is another word religion has redefined into an action we must do. Paul, however, saw it as an acknowledgment of what we already possess. We can only possess what we've already been given. Receiving doesn't trigger something to happen. Yet, religion turned it into a work we must do because it's not ours until we "receive" it. No, it's already ours *before* we receive it; we already possess it because of what Jesus finished. Receiving something means recognizing that we already have it. He's already given us all things that pertain to life and godliness. All things already belong to us, and we are meant to lay hold and claim them as if they are already ours! That's receiving.

> Receiving doesn't prompt God to give it to us; it affirms what we already possess in Christ.

Now that we have gained a clearer understanding of these four words — *confession, believing, faith, and receiving* — let's dive back into Galatians 3.

A Legacy of Grace: Unlocking God's Covenant with Abraham

> **Galatians 3:15-18:** *"Brethren, I speak in the manner of men: Though it is only a man's covenant, yet if it is confirmed, no one annuls or adds to it. Now to*

Abraham and his Seed were the promises made. He does not say, 'And to seeds,' as of many, but as of one, 'And to your Seed,' who is Christ. And this I say, that the law, which was four hundred and thirty years later, cannot annul the covenant that was confirmed before by God in Christ, that it should make the promise of no effect. For if the inheritance is of the law, it is no longer of promise; but God gave it to Abraham by promise.'"

The inheritance didn't come through the law. It was through the promise. Paul goes on to inform us that the Law served a specific purpose.

Verses 19-25: *"What purpose then does the law serve? It was added because of transgressions, till the Seed should come to whom the promise was made; and it was appointed through angels by the hand of a mediator. Now a mediator does not mediate for one only, but God is one. Is the law then against the promises of God? Certainly not! For if there had been a law given which could have given life, truly righteousness would have been by the law. But the Scripture has confined all under sin, that the promise by faith in Jesus Christ might be given to those who believe. But before faith came, we were kept under guard by the law, kept for the faith which would afterward be revealed. Therefore the law was our tutor to bring us to Christ, that we might be justified by*

> *faith. But after faith has come, we are no longer under a tutor."*

The sole purpose of the Law was to reveal to them that they couldn't attain God's favor through obeying the Law; they fell short in their attempts to follow it. Its entire objective was to direct their attention to the necessity of a Savior. Gentiles were never under the Law. And after the cross, no one (including Jews) was under the Law. Romans 10:4 declares that to everyone who believes, Christ is the end of the Law. He entirely fulfilled it *as us*.

> The final part of **chapter 3, verses 26-29:** *"For you are all sons of God through faith in Christ Jesus. For as many of you as were baptized into Christ have put on Christ. There is neither Jew nor Greek, there is neither slave nor free, there is neither male nor female; for you are all one in Christ Jesus. And if you are Christ's, then you are Abraham's seed, and heirs according to the promise."*

Paul states that now, in Christ, we all share in the inheritance and are heirs of every promise God made to Abraham. The promise to Abraham was that he would experience divine favor in all his endeavors and possess the land wherever he set foot. Moreover, through him, all the nations of the world would be blessed. Paul emphasizes to the Galatians that the Law had no bearing on God's covenant with Abraham. God made a promise to Abraham 430 years before the Law.

> The Law didn't nullify God's covenant with Abraham; it was a parenthesis in history given to Abraham with its fulfillment realized through the Seed, who is Christ.

Moving Forward: The Path to Sonship in Grace

In chapter four, Paul takes a dramatic shift and begins to teach them about the progression of sonship, which we will explore in part two of this book (chapters 8-14). As we conclude this first part of the book, it's crucial to grasp chapters one, two, and three accurately. In summary, Paul initiated the letter by establishing the cornerstone of his message: Jesus plus nothing! He made no additions to the Gospel directly revealed by Jesus, and Paul condemns any attempt to add to it as a counterfeit gospel.

In chapter two, he dismantles everything that has restrained and sought to confine us, preventing us from moving forward. Paul encourages us to shed the beliefs of needing to earn God's favor and merit His blessings. Then, in chapter three, Paul confronts them by asking, "Hey, you foolish Galatians, you who began in grace, why are you trying to perfect yourselves through the law? Are you so senseless that after starting in the Spirit, you believe you can be perfected through the flesh?"

In the first three chapters of Galatians, Paul effectively reveals the barriers that hinder and stop our personal growth, encouraging them to eliminate that performance-based mentality and stop mixing law with grace. In chapters four, five, and six, he will guide them (AND US) in moving forward and maturing as sons, grounded in grace rather than religion and the religious activity of doing to become.

Part Two

Manifested Sonship: The Grace Journey Continues

Chapter 8

Embracing Sonship and Authority

How we perceive ourselves in the private moments when it's just us and we've taken off the masks plays a pivotal role in shaping our daily lives. The truth of our identity was established by the Father in Christ before the foundation of the world. He created us in His image and likeness, breathing the breath of life into our very being.

Our lost sense of our true identity began with Adam's decision, which ushered humanity through the door of forgetfulness. We suffered from amnesia, and regrettably, the church often failed to assist us in recovering who we are in Christ. Instead, it reinforced a false narrative that we were separated from God and alienated from His goodness. Then, in the fullness of time, Jesus stepped in, His purpose being to awaken us to the truth of our eternal identity. He came to jog our memory, to transform how we see ourselves.

Unveiling the Mystery: Christ in You

Paul carried the revelation of our identity in Christ to the Gentiles. In Colossians 1:26, Paul states that the mystery of the Gospel concealed throughout the ages and generations has now been revealed to the saints. What was the mystery? Verse 27 says, "To them God willed to make known what are the riches of the glory of this mystery among the Gentiles: which is Christ in you, the hope of glory." The hope of glory is the complete realization of the Christ who has always resided within us, even if we failed to recognize it. It was a concealed mystery, unveiled two thousand years ago.

If this revelation was shared with the saints two millennia ago, it stands to reason that it should shine even brighter for today's saints. Yet, it seems that the church frequently veils this truth from us, substituting it with a narrative that our identity is broken and distorted and separated from God.

In the first three chapters of Galatians, Paul passionately encouraged the believers to forsake the false identity and the works-based gospel of law and behavior modification. He guided them back into the powerful revelation that caused him to break all ties with religion, which is simply Jesus plus nothing. It's pure grace with no legalism, conditions, or strings attached.

It's the complete sufficiency of everything Jesus

accomplished for us and as us. Our true identity is Christ in us.

From Child Heirs to Mature Sons

> **Galatians 4:1-7:** *"Now I say that the heir, as long as he is a child, does not differ at all from a slave, though he is master of all, but is under guardians and stewards until the time appointed by the father. Even so we, when we were children, were in bondage under the elements of the world. But when the fullness of the time had come, God sent forth His Son, born of a woman, born under the law, to redeem those who were under the law, that we might receive the adoption as sons. And because you are sons, God has sent forth the Spirit of His Son into your hearts, crying out, "Abba, Father!" Therefore you are no longer a slave but a son, and if a son, then an heir of God through Christ."*

In the passage above, Paul highlights three distinct roles: that of a child, a servant, and a son. **Our calling is not to be servants but to embrace sonship.** It's the sons who experience true freedom, fulfillment, and purpose. Unfortunately, the concept of sonship hasn't been emphasized much in the church because religious systems often focus on keeping people in servitude. Most evangelical churches teach how to be a servant, but that's not your true identity.

The motivations and perspectives of servants and sons are markedly different. Let's draw an analogy: Imagine your family owns a substantial business, and one day, you're destined to take the reins of that family enterprise. Right now, your father has complete control, but he's well aware that it will be your responsibility one day. This perspective sets you apart from an ordinary employee. You have a higher calling — that of sonship.

Romans 8:19 reminds us that all of creation eagerly anticipates the manifestation of the sons of God. **The world isn't seeking more servants; it's searching for sons, those who have reached the full maturity of sonship**.

If your family owns that large business, the son is deeply invested in the family enterprise. In contrast, the servants or employees working in the same business are solely focused on one thing: their wages. They are only interested in the minimum work required to get paid. However, the owner's son has a different outlook; his work ethic differs from a servants. The business is his inheritance; he has a vested interest in it. A servant has no share in the business's inheritance.

Paul explains that a child heir possesses immense potential but actually possesses nothing more than the servant. He's a son in the making but still immature. This is where many of us have found ourselves stuck and frustrated in the kingdom of God. We've been like the child heirs, and what we've manifested has been nothing different than the servant. As sons, we have great potential, but as my father wisely shared, potential alone signifies that you haven't yet taken action. A child heir may have great potential, but they lack actual possession due to immaturity.

Paul further describes how this child heir is under the guidance of governors and tutors. Just like a governor on a car controls its speed, these tutors are responsible for determining how rapidly this child heir progresses based on their level of maturity. If everything goes as planned, there will come a time when this child heir is deemed ready to step into their entire inheritance. The moment arrives when the father feels confident that the child heir has matured enough to transition into sonship. In this stage, they can reflect the father's character, take charge of the family business, and carry out their responsibilities with the same mindset as the father. The father can release control and say, "I've completed my role in governing the kingdom and managing the business. It's now in your capable hands."

The Shift from Servants to Manifested Sons

I have a strong sense that the time of God's sovereign intervention is drawing to a close, and He is transitioning responsibility to the sons who are actively manifesting the work of the kingdom. Up to this point, the Father had to handle much of this work himself because we were still child heirs, possessing potential but lacking actual ownership. We remained under the guidance of governors and tutors, and many of us experienced stunted growth due to the constraints of the religious system we were under. This system failed to adequately nurture and guide us, holding us back from the progress we could have made.

In Philippians, chapter 2, Paul sheds light on this concept. Philippians 2:5-6 states, "Let this mind be in you which was also in Christ Jesus, who, being in the form of God, did not consider it robbery to be equal with God" It is the mindset we must adopt, one where we feel equal to God. Jesus embodied this, and as He is, so are we in this world.

As you grow into the measure of the stature of the fullness of Christ, you begin to walk as if the Father Himself were walking. As a manifested son, you operate in the kingdom and its fullness as though the Father were personally managing the business. The Father is not seeking servants. While you might have been taught in church to serve tirelessly, the Father's intention isn't to have servants who begrudgingly fulfill their duties, always pondering the minimum effort required. This mentality can often emerge in church settings, where the prevailing thought becomes, *what's the bare minimum I must do to fulfill this task?*

The Father is not raising servants but building a strong company of sons fully aware of their sonship. They are growing into complete readiness, ensuring they are equipped for any role within the kingdom. These sons possess the necessary qualifications and carry a willing heart to serve. Mirroring the way Jesus lived. He was fully conscious of His Sonship by position. However, in his outward appearance and actions, He was a servant. Jesus told His disciples that He didn't come to be ministered to but to minister. He didn't come to be served but to serve. This statement flowed from His deep understanding of His identity as a Son.

Paul explains that every person whom God foreknew, He predestined to be conformed to the image of His Son. Therefore, all of us are undergoing a transformation, much like clay on a potter's wheel. The Father is shaping us into the same image, instilling in us the same mindset, mentality, outlook, and perception that Jesus embodies.

A servant's mindset is fundamentally different from that of a son. A servant lacks the rights, position, and authority that a son possesses. A servant is more focused on personal desires and objectives. In contrast, a son profoundly cares about the Father's interests. A son works in union with the Father.

> The critical distinction between a son and a servant is that a son has the law of the Father written in his heart, while a servant has it stored in his head.

Consequently, a son's actions originate from a heart that intimately knows the Father's heart, granting him a sense of rest and security. So, Jesus approached His work with the heart of a servant, all the while knowing His position as a Son in the Father's kingdom.

In John 5, Jesus unveils the heart that stems from the sonship that Paul was leading the Galatians into. He cleared away all religious activity, works, and efforts in the first three chapters and introduced them to the mindset of Jesus plus nothing. What was the mindset of Jesus? Son by position and servant by manifestation. In John 5:19-20, Jesus said, "Most assuredly, I say to you, the Son can do nothing of Himself, but what He sees the Father do; for whatever He does, the Son also does in like manner. For the Father loves the Son, and shows Him all things that He Himself does; and He will show Him greater works than these, that you may marvel."

Then, in Galatians 4, Paul takes a significant turn in his discussion. Up to this point, he has been addressing the concepts of child heirs and servants, examining who possesses and who doesn't, who holds a position and who doesn't. In verses 4-5, he states, "But when the fullness of the time had come, God sent forth His Son, born of a woman, born under the law, to redeem those who were under the law, that we might receive the adoption as sons." Our adoption into sonship is the same one Jesus experienced. In verse 6, Paul further emphasizes, "And because you are sons, God has sent forth the Spirit of His Son into your hearts, crying out, 'Abba, Father!'" It signifies an intimate working relationship and a place in the family business, just as Jesus had.

> **However, there is a timing, a fullness of time, that must come.**

Jesus, too, had to wait for the appointed time. As a man, perhaps at 18, He thought He was ready, having received a vision and a mission in His heart. By 25, maybe He wondered when it would happen. By 28, He may have questioned whether He missed God or did something wrong. But He chose to trust the Father because He knows where we are in the maturing process and how much to release into our hands. This journey is a marathon, not a sprint. You might feel frustrated, thinking you're not progressing or stuck for too long. However, you are right where you need to be now, at this juncture. You are in a perfect position.

The release came for Jesus when He was 30 and not a moment before. Your release will come. You are further along in the kingdom than you realize and have made more progress than you think. You might not be seeing yourself through the eyes of the Father, but you are more prepared than you think. The day of the company of manifesting sons is at the door. It's not a distant future event or tied to something like the rapture. It's right here, knocking at your door.

Religion has instilled a servant mentality, focusing on doing the bare minimum. It has framed the narrative around who goes to heaven and who goes to an illusionary place of hell to be consciously tormented eternally. It has emphasized serving in hopes of hearing God say, "Well done, good and faithful servant." But is that what He will genuinely say? No. He will declare, "This is My son in whom I am well pleased!" We must shift from this servant mindset to one of sonship. Religion has held people back, keeping them in a servanthood mentality when they should be taught how to manifest as sons. It contradicts the purpose of the five-fold ministry in the church.

> **Ephesians 4:10-13 elaborates on this:** *"He who descended is also the One who ascended far above all the heavens, that He might fill all things.) And He Himself gave some to be apostles, some prophets, some evangelists, and some pastors and teachers, for the equipping of the saints for the work of ministry, for the edifying of the body of Christ, till we all come to the unity of the faith and of the knowledge of the Son of God, to a perfect man, to the measure of the stature of the fullness of Christ;"*

The goal of the five-fold ministry is to bring all to the unity of the faith and the knowledge of the Son of God, to a perfect man, to the measure of the stature of the fullness of Christ. But the church has fallen short of this goal. Instead of teaching people how to be servants of God, the church should have been teaching about the manifestation of sons. The world is not seeking the manifestation of servants; it's eagerly anticipating the demonstration of fully mature sons of God, operating at their fullest potential, making a difference, and living out their sonship.

THE DIVINE TRANSITION: BECOMING A MANIFESTED SONSHIP

The purpose of Jesus, as Paul described in Galatians 4:4-5, was to bring us into sonship. Before He was released into that purpose, Jesus didn't perform miracles, raise the dead, or walk on water because He was under the guidance of tutors and governors, including His parents and the Holy Spirit. When the transition from a child-heir to a son happened, He was released into His mission: to usher us into sonship.

Was Jesus the Son of God at ages 15, 20, and 25? Yes, He embodied the fullness of the Godhead in bodily form. Still, there was a specific moment when He became fully conscious of His identity. In Luke 3:22, after His baptism, the Holy Spirit descended like a dove, and a voice from heaven declared, "You are My beloved Son; in You, I am well pleased." This was the moment of His release into manifested sonship.

There is a distinct moment when you transition from being a child-heir to walking in the manifestation of sonship. Jesus, filled with the Spirit, proclaimed His mission in Luke 4:17, which included preaching the Gospel, healing the brokenhearted, liberating the oppressed, and proclaiming the acceptable year of the Lord, Jubilee, where all that was lost is restored. He also promised in John 14:12 that those who believe in Him will do greater works because He was going to the Father. 1 John 4:17 emphasizes that we are to be in this present world as He is. You'll experience a shift where what was impossible yesterday becomes possible today. The words that used to fall to the ground without having any effect will now open blind eyes and heal the sick. You'll consistently walk out the reality of Luke 4:17-18, performing miraculous acts one after another.

Isaiah foresaw it, saying, *"Arise, shine; For your light has come! And the glory of the Lord is risen upon you. For behold, the darkness shall cover the earth, And deep darkness the people; But the Lord will arise over you, And His glory will be seen upon you. The Gentiles shall come to your light, And kings to the brightness of your rising. Lift up your eyes all around, and see: They all gather together, they come to you; Your sons shall come from afar, And your daughters shall be nursed at your side. Then you shall see and become radiant, And your heart shall swell with joy; Because the abundance of the sea shall be turned to you, The wealth of the Gentiles shall come to you. The multitude of camels shall cover your* land, *The dromedaries of Midian and Ephah; All those from Sheba shall come; They shall bring gold and incense, And they shall proclaim the praises of the Lord."*
(ISAIAH 60:1-6)

Isaiah's vision from the past mirrors what I see today. Jesus is the Light that illuminates every person in the world. There's no need to chase people down with the good news, just as Jesus never did. They will come to you; they will find you. Arise and shine, for your light has come. It's your light that draws them. There is no need to go out and evangelize, pursuing people to make confessions or say prayers. We see in Mark 6:31 that Jesus had so many people flocking to Him that there wasn't even time to eat. The modern-day church often uses elaborate marketing plans, brochures, and television programs to attract people. Jesus didn't employ such tactics. It was what radiated from within Him that drew people in. The same is true for you. The life of Christ in you will draw people.

The passage in Galatians 4:1-7 is often overlooked, and we haven't drawn much out of it. The Father has instilled the heart of a son with you. As long as you live under any law, you find yourself in a servant's role, constantly bowing your knee, performing, striving, and attempting to please the master (which is the law).

What set Jesus apart from everyone around Him? He consistently did what pleased the Father. He never refused the Father's will but carried out His work as the Father intended. In return, the Father never denied Him. Jesus did not lead a life of choices, nor are we meant to. **We are to live as Jesus did — responding to the Father's guidance. We are to follow where the Father leads, just as Jesus did.** The tree of the knowledge of good and evil symbolizes the law's temptation to choose, but a son does not need to strive to obey or make choices. Instead, a son responds out of unity and love, intimately knowing the Father's heart.

Galatians 4:7 wraps it all up beautifully. Paul states, "Therefore you are no longer a slave but a son, and if a son, then an heir of God through Christ." You are not a servant to the law's demands. You carry the mark of sonship, bestowed upon you *even before the foundation of the world.*

The Power of Adoption

In verse 5, the term "adoption" is significant. In Roman society, an adopted child had a special status. You could disown a natural child, but an adopted child was irrevocably part of the family. They held full family standing and could act on behalf of the father who adopted them, essentially possessing power of attorney. Paul's message is clear: we are sons who act on behalf of the Father, and the Father supports our actions when we live not by making choices but by responding.

If you have seen yourself as a servant, it's time to embrace the spirit of adoption that rightfully belongs to you. You can act fully on behalf of the Father because you are a co-heir with Jesus. Clinging to the servant mentality holds you back. You are a son.

Again, the journey of rediscovering your true identity in Christ is a marathon, not a sprint.

There are seasons of preparation, much like Paul's 14 years maturing in the revelation of grace. **We may feel unready, but we are more prepared than we realize.** The revelation of grace, of Jesus plus nothing, is taking root. As we refuse to compromise on the complete inclusion of all humanity revealed in the Gospel, we draw closer to manifesting as sons. This Gospel renews our minds and lives. Be assured you are right where you need to be in the process.

Chapter 9

Unveiling Sonship's Four Stages

This chapter takes a fresh perspective on understanding the stages of sonship, where we journey from child-heir to fully manifested son. It's essential to grasp that our empowerment to become fully mature sons of God does not lie in our strength or abilities; God orchestrates it.

The Crucible of Sonship: Growth and Patience

The journey of sonship unfolds through distinct stages, which are frequently misunderstood. Understanding these stages is crucial for practical cooperation with them. As my friend Sheila Begley pointed out in a Facebook post, our Christ identity isn't something we can merely conceptualize. In other words, our identity isn't theoretical. To truly experience our union with God, we must yield to the ongoing process and daily learn to submit to the Christ within us.

The Father's ultimate goal is the complete manifestation of His sons. In simple terms, this means becoming as Jesus is in this present world. If you lack an understanding of the sonship process and a readiness to embrace it, you may grow weary as He shapes you, and there's a risk of giving up during the maturation process. When the Father deals with us, His purpose is not to bring about condemnation or guilt but rather to provide discipline.

> Sonship development is intricately tied to character growth and the cultivation of patience.

Patience is produced by facing situations that challenge our consistency under pressure. The Father permits circumstances in our lives that create pressure, and His desire is for you to learn to remain resolute in challenging situations.

Jesus remained consistent under pressure. During a storm, while all the disciples were frantically bailing water out of the boat to save themselves and prevent it from sinking, Jesus remained peacefully asleep. For 30 years, He learned obedience through challenges and opposition to bring Him to the place of full release from the Father. Just because we walk in grace and believe in grace doesn't mean that life won't present us with challenges and opposition. 1 Peter 4:12 states, "Beloved, do not think it strange concerning the fiery trial which is to try you, as though some strange thing happened to you;" Peter emphasizes that it's unusual if you don't endure these fiery trials. **These challenges are indicators of our progress in this journey of maturing as sons.** You will encounter situations that bring adversity, but the key distinction is how grace empowers you to handle the trials that come your way in life.

Embracing Divine Discipline

In Hebrews 12:5, it is written, "And you have forgotten the exhortation which speaks to you as to sons: 'My son, do not despise the chastening of the Lord, nor be discouraged when you are rebuked by Him.'" Take a moment to underline the word "despise" in your Bible. Verse 6 states, "For whom the Lord loves, He chastens, and scourges every son whom He receives."

> **It's important to clarify that "scourge" doesn't imply that God inflicts sickness or disease upon you.** Instead, it signifies His willingness to guide and discipline you in the right direction.

Verse 7 further reinforces this, "If you endure chastening, God deals with you as with sons; for what son is there whom a father does not chasten?" Verse 8 tells us that without discipline, we are illegitimate. We are disciplined because we are sons. The author of Hebrews outlines three possible responses to God's discipline in Hebrews 12.

- The first is to despise it, which means feeling contempt, disdain, or reacting with anger and upset.
- The second is becoming discouraged, leading to feelings of fainting, giving up, walking away, or even depression.
- The third, which is encouraged, is endurance. It involves yielding and undergoing the process, walking in obedience as the Father desires.

In Galatians 4:1-7, Paul discusses the shift from being a child heir to becoming a mature son. This transformation unfolds through discipline, life's circumstances, nurturing, and personal growth. Rather than resisting these experiences, we must welcome and submit to this ongoing process. The Father has a distinct goal in mind — the manifestation of the sons of God on Earth, each one with a particular purpose, echoing what Jesus emphasized in Matthew chapter 24.

> Matthew 24:14 states, *"And this gospel of the kingdom will be preached in all the world as a witness to all the nations, and then the end will come."*

Preaching the Gospel doesn't solely involve standing at a pulpit or addressing a large audience. It's about establishing a standard on Earth, enabling every earthly kingdom to be assessed by its alignment with the Kingdom standard. This task falls to the sons of God, who will introduce His Kingdom and bring other domains under its influence. In entertainment, sports, news media, or any other sphere, the sons of God will be strategically placed to raise this standard and manifest their sonship, advancing the Kingdom's presence in these various dimensions. Essentially, they will act as living witnesses, representing the good news of the Kingdom, preaching it, ministering it, and demonstrating it globally. And this mission will be carried out by the manifested sons of God.

Paul's message in Romans 8:19 becomes apparent when he states, "For the earnest expectation of the creation eagerly waits for the revealing of the sons of God." All creation is on the edge of its seat, yearning for the manifestation of genuine sons of God. It's searching for those who have undergone a transformative journey and can represent Christ in this world, setting the standard for the Kingdom. You will be the Christ they encounter, demonstrating the Kingdom's standard. **The entirety of creation anticipates your role in this with great eagerness.**

There are four distinct stages of sonship to consider as steps in the transformation process. The journey starts with *neipos*, advances to *paidion*, then *teknon*, and ultimately arrives at *huios*. Though the journey varies for each person, every step is crucial. If you despise or become discouraged during this journey, you might find yourself in a situation where you've been a follower of Jesus for twenty years but have yet to mature significantly, essentially repeating the same year of growth twenty times over. God's aim is for your maturation.

What I'm sharing with you has not only been a great help in my own life as I discovered these stages of development, but it has also provided me with insight into why some individuals remain stuck as child heirs and fail to mature. When God disciplines us, we sometimes shift blame onto external factors like the devil or other people's actions. Alternatively, we become disheartened, sulk, leave, or refuse to endure, failing to release whatever is holding us back.

Sometimes, we expect people to exhibit a higher level of sonship than they can at a given moment. It's essential to be patient and allow individuals to grow in grace and maturity. Let's explore each stage.

Stage One - *NEIPOS*: Spiritual Babyhood

Galatians 4:1 states that "… the heir, as long as he is a child, does not differ at all from a slave, though he is master of all… ." Despite having immense potential, a child heir doesn't yet possess what is rightfully theirs because they are still children. The word used to describe this stage is the Greek word *neipos*. *Neipos* refers to someone from birth to about two years old — a beginner, a new convert, someone awakening to the truth, a person characterized by innocence and simplicity. It's akin to that baby you bring home from the hospital who grows and learns how to walk.

Let's look some scriptures where the term *neipos* is used.

> Ephesians 4:14 states, *"That we should no longer be children (neipos), tossed to and fro and carried about with every wind of doctrine, by the trickery of men, in the cunning craftiness of deceitful plotting."*

Lack of stability characterizes *neipos*. They tend to be easily swayed by different teachings and can fall for trickery and deceit. They're beginning their spiritual journey.

> In 1 Corinthians 13:11, Paul says, *"When I was a child (neipos), I spoke as a child, I understood as a child, I thought as a child; but when I became a man, I put away childish things."*

This passage emphasizes the importance of growth and development. Like a child outgrowing their childish behaviors, our spiritual journey involves a growth process.

In the natural world, infants or *neipos* don't have jobs or chores; they eat, sleep, and need care. In the spiritual realm, *neipos* are just opening their eyes to an entirely new dimension. They are filled with enthusiasm and love for everyone they encounter. We should allow them to be like that because it's a beautiful discovery stage.

However, a problem arises in the church when *neipos*, despite their age and talents, are pushed into positions of authority or responsibility prematurely. They should be allowed to grow and develop naturally. Just as it's normal for a six-month-old baby to wear diapers, when that child reaches the age of around ten, you certainly wouldn't want them to still be in diapers. Just as a child progresses beyond infancy, we should advance beyond the baby stage into the next development phase.

So, if you find yourself in the *neipos* stage, savor God's grace and unconditional love that you've recently discovered. The Father offers you plenty of grace during this period. Plant your feet firmly, gain understanding, and develop. As you grow and mature, remember that there's more to discover and learn on your journey.

Stage Two - *PAIDION*: Childlike Sons

The next stage of development is called *paidion*, covering the age range from about two to 12 years, corresponding to young childhood. In John chapter 21, Jesus used this term when addressing the disciples in John 21:5-6. He said, "Then Jesus said to them, 'Children, have you any food?' They answered Him, 'No.' And He said to them, 'Cast the net on the right side of the boat, and you will find some.' So they cast, and now they were not able to draw it in because of the multitude of fish." Here, Jesus referred to them as *paidions*.

This stage is marked by significant growth. You've likely observed rapid changes and growth spurts if you've raised children in this age group. In just one summer, they grow fast, and their clothes suddenly become too short or small, like what we used to call "floods."

As we transition through this phase, discipline and oversight are crucial in the natural and spiritual realms. It's a significant period where parents need to allow their young children to learn certain things independently, even if it means they have to experience specific lessons, like the stove being hot, firsthand, despite warnings.

Paidions can be demanding, whether in the natural or spiritual realm. They tend to assert their own way and become upset when they can't have candy before dinner, throwing fits when denied. Spiritually, they might think they understand more than they actually do, often remaining heavily dependent on the church. In a way, the church sometimes prefers to keep individuals in this *paidion* stage where they rely on the church for guidance.

Interestingly, in John chapter 21, Jesus asked the disciples if they had anything to eat, to which they replied, "No." Instead of performing a miracle to provide them with food, such as a fish, Jesus took a different approach. He taught them how to fish, a significant step in their development. Until then, the disciples had relied on Jesus to provide for their needs. However, He instructed them to take care of it themselves this time. This story mirrors the process during the *paidion* stage, where parents or mentors assist the child's development. However, in some cases within the church, there's a tendency to keep individuals dependent rather than allowing them to progress beyond this stage.

In the spiritual sense, *paidions* lack deep insight due to their stage of development. Consequently, *paidions* gravitate towards specific teachers, often following them closely and becoming somewhat fixated on their teachings. It isn't necessarily part of God's design, as His plan is for continual growth.

Because they possess only limited spiritual insight, *paidions* are predominantly influenced by their emotions and intellect. They echo the words of their chosen teacher, the beliefs of their church, or what they've read, often proclaiming their church as the best or the only one, akin to children arguing about their fathers' strength in an imaginary contest.

Paidions haven't fully discovered their identity, and they're still figuring it out. After repeatedly sitting in church for years and hearing the same message, they rarely question it and firmly hold onto what they believe. One key characteristic of *paidions* is their aversion to correction and dislike being told "no." Also, they are prone to significant mood swings.

This stage in sonship development is critical because one must choose whether to continue growing or become stuck. Some individuals do get trapped at this stage, remaining immature. They acquire enough knowledge to repeat what others have said or uphold their church's doctrines, but they never progress beyond this point.

In 1 Corinthians 14:20, *paidion* and *neipos* are mentioned. The verse states, "Brethren, do not be children (*paidion*) in understanding; however, in malice be babes (*neipos*), but in understanding be mature." Here, Paul advises them to move beyond the stage of *paidion* in their understanding. They continually require instruction, knowledge, and understanding. Their spiritual life remains underdeveloped, and their soul (mind, will, and emotions) tends to dominate their actions.

When the Father disciplines, *paidions* often react based on their emotions, becoming upset. They tend to despise or become discouraged, typically showing disdain when faced with the Father's discipline. They might get angry and deflect blame, often attributing their actions to external factors like the devil, much like the classic line, "the devil made me do it." *Paidions* struggle to take responsibility, which hinders the transformative change that the Father aims to bring into their lives for continued growth and maturation.

Stage Three - TEKNON: The Teenage Phase

The third stage is where the real transformation occurs. Now, you're transitioning from being driven by your soulish tendencies to becoming more spirit-led. This third stage is called *teknon*, similar to the teenage years. Ephesians 5:1 tells us to "be imitators of God as dear children," using the word *teknon*. Paul is addressing individuals who are akin to teenagers in their spiritual journey.

Think of a teenager in the natural sense. You might see a 15 or 16-year-old boy who's 6 foot 2 and weighs 210 pounds, looking like a full-grown man. However, emotionally and in terms of understanding, he's still 15 or 16. The same applies to *teknons* spiritually; they may look mature outwardly, but emotionally and spiritually, they still need to fully develop as sons. They are progressing through this stage and the associated process.

Naturally, teenagers often make decisions based on their emotions. Emotions play a significant role in their lives, and they can easily be offended or rejected. Insecurity is common among teenagers, who constantly need affirmation and encouragement. Striking a balance between building them up and preventing them from becoming ego-driven is crucial.

Teenagers can be challenging; they're quick to express their thoughts and opinions, even if those opinions might not have a solid basis. As a parent, you understand they may not fully grasp the situation, but they genuinely believe in their viewpoints. This same characteristic applies spiritually during the *teknon* phase.

Let me provide a couple of illustrations from the life of Peter to help you understand what a *teknon* looks like. In Mark 8:31-33, it's written, "And He began to teach them that the Son of Man must suffer many things, and be rejected by the elders and chief priests and scribes, and be killed, and after three days rise again. He spoke this word openly. Then Peter took Him aside and began to rebuke Him. But when He had turned around and looked at His disciples, He rebuked Peter, saying, 'Get behind Me, Satan! For you are not mindful of the things of God, but the things of men.'"

Was Peter speaking from a place where he believed he had the best intentions? Absolutely! Peter was sharing his opinion. Can you imagine — Peter is pulling God aside and rebuking Him!? So Jesus looks at him and says, "Satan, get behind me." Was Peter Satan? Of course not. Jesus essentially tells Peter, "You have no idea what you're talking about. Your focus is on the things of men, not the things of God." Peter thought he was aligning with the will of God by trying to protect Jesus, but Jesus made it clear that Peter's understanding was way off. Peter's reactions throughout the Gospels are a prime example of how a *teknon* behaves.

A story from Matthew chapter 17 perfectly illustrates how a *teknon* behaves. After six days, Jesus took Peter, James, and John to a high mountain by themselves. While they were there, Jesus was transfigured before them. His face began to shine like the sun, and his clothes became as white as light. To add to the surreal scene, Moses and Elijah suddenly appeared and were in conversation with Jesus. If I were in that situation, I would be completely speechless. I'd absorb the moment, not knowing how to put it into words. But not Peter, not a *teknon*.

Peter always has something to say and an opinion, even when no one asks. He boldly suggests, "Lord, it's great that we're here. Let's build three tabernacles — one for you, one for Moses, and one for Elijah." And he keeps talking and talking. But then, in verse five, something incredible happens. While Peter was still speaking, a bright cloud overshadowed them, and a voice emerged from the cloud, saying, "This is my beloved Son, in whom I'm well pleased. Listen to Him!"

The disciples fell to the ground in fear. Jesus, in his gentle way, reassured them. It's an incredible scene. Picture it: Jesus transfigured, Moses and Elijah appeared, and Peter chatted away without a care. A *teknon*, much like a teenager, is never hesitant to share their thoughts, even if it's a bit out of place. It's like a moment of embarrassment for Peter, and God intervenes to remind them all that it's about Jesus, not the emphasis on Elijah or Moses, who were there to represent the prophets and the law. The spotlight is on Jesus.

Another time, Jesus asked His disciples, "Who do men say that I am?" Peter confidently responds, "Thou art the Christ, the Son of the Living God." Jesus commends him, saying, "Peter, that's amazing! Man has not revealed that to you; you received it directly from heaven." I can picture Peter beaming with pride, chest puffed out. But the very next day, Peter wants to cut off a soldier's ear and insists that Jesus shouldn't go to the cross. Do you see the wavering happening here? *Teknons* can act mature one day and regress to behaving like a *paidion* the next. Isn't it reassuring that John wrote in John 1:12 that we are in the process of becoming? *Teknons* can be quite ego-driven, full of pride and selfishness one moment, and the next, they do something that makes you believe they're all grown up. That's the nature of teenagers.

I used these verses to give you a broad picture of what the *teknon* stage looks like. Some of you might be reading this and thinking, *I've been like this. I often let my emotions guide me. I'm starting to grasp spiritual things, but I'm constantly pulled back by my feelings, and my mind seems to be at odds with my journey. My will is strong, and it often pushes me in its direction.* That's okay; you might find yourself at the *teknon* stage of development. Or some of you may still be in the *paidion* or *neipos* stages, and that's perfectly fine because God is empowering you to become the manifested sons of God.

Stage Four - HUIOS: The Maturity of Manifested Sonship

The Father is leading us toward maturity, the fourth stage of development called *huios*. Romans chapter 8:14 states, "For as many as are led by the Spirit of God, these are sons (*huios*) of God." Furthermore, Romans 8:19 tells us that all of creation eagerly anticipates the manifestation of the sons (*huios*) of God. **Huios are the mature sons of God, and this term is also used in Scripture when referring to Jesus.**

In this context, maturity means we operate from our spirit, not our soul. *Huios* are submitted to God, they take on responsibility, they no longer identify as servants but as sons, and they fully understand their position. *Huios* practice self-denial, exhibit patience, and speak not with their own words but what they hear the Father say. They possess all things and yet seek nothing for themselves.

Being around a *huios* is quite reassuring, much like having an older brother when you're around ten years old. You feel safe and secure, knowing that the older brother, 18, 19, or 20, won't harm you. That's how *neipos*, *paidion*, and *teknons* feel around *huios*. *Huios* are positive influences; they won't lead you into trouble because their emotions do not sway them.

You're naturally drawn to *huios* in the kingdom because they exude spiritual maturity. It is what all of creation is searching for – the *huios*. They aren't seeking *neipos*, *paidion*, or *teknons*. They want the *huios* who reflect the Father, carry out His work without hidden agendas, and aren't in competition with each other. The Kingdom competition among prophets, apostles, and churches happening today is more in line with a *teknon*, not a *huios*.

Reaching this stage of sonship maturity is the most powerful position we can attain in the earthly realm. *Huios* walk with unwavering confidence, knowing that the Father is always with them. They can reflect on their life journey and recognize how the Father's guidance has freed them from past bonds and emotional constraints. Now, they are liberated to be their authentic selves, to manifest the Father's image, and to embrace their calling.

Huios understands that the Father's business encompasses whatever they do. Whether they're school teachers, lawyers, real estate agents, factory workers, or burger flippers, it doesn't matter; the Father is involved in life with them.

In Acts 10:38, it's written, "... how God anointed Jesus of Nazareth with the Holy Spirit and with power, who went about doing good and healing all who were oppressed by the devil, for God was with Him." *Huios* carry out their daily activities; wherever they go, they do the Father's work. When we look at Jesus' life, we see a prime example of a *huios* in action.

In Luke 4:17-18, Jesus entered the temple after His baptism, signifying the sealing of His identity with the Father's affirmation. He took the book and declared, "The Spirit of the Lord is upon Me because He has anointed Me." He then listed several things, like healing the brokenhearted, setting captives free, and bringing the year of Jubilee, a year of restoration. It's a picture of *huios*, of manifested sonship. A *huios* doesn't seek validation or affirmation from others. They don't need constant confirmation of their identity because they know who they are.

As you step into your role as a son and venture into new territories, there will always be people who disapprove, no matter how dedicated and passionate you are. If you haven't undergone the discipline and training provided by the Father through the necessary process, you're likely to feel hurt and offended when you encounter disapproval, lack of recognition, or the absence of praise from others. If you're not walking in the maturity of a *huios* and find yourself at the *neipos*, *paidion*, or *teknon* stage, you might end up despising the unfolding events of your life, experiencing discouragement, and ultimately lacking the endurance required to press on.

Jesus is our ultimate example of a *huios*, balancing remarkable humility with unwavering confidence. He willingly poured out His life in service, declaring, "I didn't come to be served, but to serve." Yet, within his humility, he maintained profound confidence. He boldly stated, "I always do what pleases the Father." What a powerful statement! He affirmed His oneness with the Father, saying, "The Father and I are one," and knew that every time He prayed, the Father answered. Astonishingly, He didn't consider it as robbery to be equal with God. It's a compelling testament to both his humility and His understanding of sonship.

A *huios*, a mature son, understands that their identity is that of a son. Yet their actions are to resemble that of a servant. They carry themselves as servants outwardly, yet internally, they understand their identity as sons.

We've walked through the various stages of sonship development, mirroring children's natural growth. These stages are essential steps in your spiritual journey, from the innocence of *neipos* and the demanding assertiveness of *paidion* to the challenge of the *teknon* phase and the ultimate maturity of *huios*. Embrace the grace and love in the *neipos* stage, gain wisdom in the *paidion* phase, and navigate your emotions in the *teknon* stage.

As you progress towards *huios*, walk in maturity, confidence, and a servant's heart, as Jesus did.

No matter where you are on this journey, remember that growth takes time, and God's discipline is a sign of His love, not condemnation. As John 1:12 teaches us, God grants the power to become *huios* of God to those who embrace their identity as sons. It's His doing, we merely cooperate with the process.

Chapter 10

Breaking Religious Barriers

Paul spent the first seven verses in Galatians 4 talking about sonship. We spent the previous two chapters expounding on the servant-son principle and the progression of the stages of sonship from being immature (*nepios*) to toddlers (*paidion*), then teenagers (*teknon*), and finally mature sons (*huios*). Now, Paul is about to share more about where the Galatians are in this maturity process and what they should know as they go through this growth process. He begins by reminding them that, at one time, they lacked a correct understanding of the nature of God, and to understand who they are as sons, they must have an accurate perception of who God is.

Shattering False Perceptions: Discovering the True Nature of God

Galatians 4:8: *"But then, indeed, when you did not*

know God, you served those which by nature are not gods."

In verse 8, Paul emphasizes that there was a time when the Galatians didn't have a revelation of God's identity, character, and nature. The Spirit of Truth had not yet revealed God to them. This absence of revelation is because of preconceived and fixed ideas about God, which act as barriers that prevent a deeper understanding of God from emerging. He encourages them to break free from these preconceptions and mental bonds, as doing so will allow them to see God more clearly.

Essentially, Paul is telling them that before they came to know the true nature of God, they were unknowingly worshipping a "god" of their own creation or one shaped by the external influences around them. This "god" they served was not the true God. Preconceived ideas and teachings clouded their perceptions. Paul's message emphasizes the importance of seeking a deeper and more accurate revelation of the true nature of God.

> The Spirit of Truth is shattering the constraints of traditional beliefs that have confined our perception of the Father.

We are starting to recognize Jesus as the complete embodiment of the Father. The Old Testament did not accurately depict the Father, and Jesus came to dispel those misconceptions. Elisha,

Jeremiah, Ezekiel, and others couldn't declare, "If you've seen me, you've seen the Father," but Jesus could. Today, through Jesus, we are gaining a clearer understanding of this truth. 1 John 3:2 states, "Beloved, now we are children of God; and it has not yet been revealed what we shall be, but we know that when He is revealed, we shall be like Him, for we shall see Him as He is." The phrase "when He shall appear" isn't referring to a second coming. It means that the moment we gain a revelation of Him. At that moment, we will be like Him because we will see Him as He truly is.

Many of us have served or are still serving a god shaped by Adam's misconceptions of a false image of God. In his mind, Adam conceived a "god" he believed to be angry, judgmental, punitive, and separated from us. But did the Father ever display anger toward Adam? No. Or was the Father ever judgmental, unkind, or severe with Adam? No, He was consistently protective. The Father led Adam away from the Tree of Life in the garden, preventing him from living in a state far below His intended plan for all eternity. Was the Father ever separated from Adam? No, He was there finding Adam and guiding him out of the garden gently, not harshly throwing him out.

Unfortunately, the distorted "god" that Adam perceived in his fallen state of mind has been passed down through generations. Even today, thousands of years later, this false perception has become deeply ingrained in our minds. When someone begins to teach about the Father who resembles Jesus, it is often rejected as false, saying, "That's not God!" Is it surprising that we've had difficulties building an intimate relationship with

Adam's "god," who was not God? **The truth is, God is nearer to us than our next breath.** Jesus's words in John 14:20 are the crux of the gospel. Jesus said on that day, you'll know that I'm in the Father, and the Father is in me, and I'm in you. The Father and the Son and all of us are all intertwined. We are in union as one together. Does this sound like the "god" Adam crafted in his mind —angry, judgmental, punitive, and distant?

Paul tells them that before they knew God, they worshiped things that weren't actually God. They were into paganism, like worshiping trees, wind, sky, moon, and stars, worshipping creation rather than the Creator.

> **Verse 9:** *"But now after you have known God, or rather are known by God, how is it that you turn again to the weak and beggarly elements, to which you desire again to be in bondage?"*

We've come to know who God is, understanding that He is the Father of everyone. Ephesians 4:6 states that there is one God and Father who is above all, through all, and in all. Sadly, though, many people in churches today are unaware that He is the Father of all. They believe He's only the Father of those who share their beliefs or have followed specific rituals like prayer, baptism, or speaking in tongues. But Paul's message is clear: He is the Father of all, above all, through all, and in all. Regardless of whether you recognize Him as such, that's who He is. Still, it's incredibly beneficial to acknowledge His true identity and live in that revelation.

Paul tells the Galatians that they've made a two-fold discovery. Not only have they found out who God is, but they've also realized that He has always known and seen them. They now see themselves the way He has always seen them, which opens the door to tremendous revelation.

Embracing Freedom: Liberating Your Faith from Religious Rituals

> **Verse 10:** *"You observe days and months and seasons and years."*

When we adopt man-made standards, we also embrace a man-made "god" who demands that we adhere to these imposed standards. God never intended to rule us through laws. That was never His plan. He never desired animal or blood sacrifices. Psalm 51:16 David said, "For you do not desire sacrifice, or else I would give *it*. You do not delight in burnt offerings." It was humanity, not God, who sought such offerings.

Consider the story at Mount Sinai, where the children of Israel rejected God's invitation to come up and know Him, preferring that Moses go on their behalf. Their reluctance gave birth to the Law. Men felt the need for animal sacrifices to cleanse their conscience and assure them that they were in right standing with God, but this was not a necessity from God's perspective.

> Jesus simplified everything by emphasizing that love is the key.

When we wholeheartedly love God, something remarkable occurs — we naturally extend that love to our neighbors. As we nurture our love for the Father, His love becomes a part of us, leading to a natural outpouring of love toward our neighbors. God-love transcends the complexities of the law and prophetic teachings.

GRACE VS. RELIGION: ZEALOUS PURSUIT OF TRUTH

> **Verses 12-15:** *"Brethren, I urge you to become like me, for I became like you. You have not injured me at all. You know that because of physical infirmity I preached the gospel to you at the first. And my trial which was in my flesh you did not despise or reject, but you received me as an angel of God, even as Christ Jesus. What then was the blessing you enjoyed? For I bear you witness that, if possible, you would have plucked out your own eyes and given them to me."*

In verses 12-15, Paul acknowledges the intense, mutual relationship they once shared. They had supported him, and he, likewise, held them in high regard. They welcomed him in the same way they would receive Christ Jesus Himself. They had walked together in elevated spiritual realms and had uncovered profound revelations. Paul had shared revelatory truths with them, and they had wholeheartedly accepted his teachings.

> **Verses 16-17:** *"Have I therefore become your enemy because I tell you the truth? They zealously court you, but for no good; yes, they want to exclude you, that you may be zealous for them.*

However, as we progress to verses 16-17, their relationship changes. Paul has become their adversary. Religion crept in and accused Paul of not disclosing the complete truth because they believed there were specific laws they must adhere to. These requirements included circumcision, obeying the Mosaic Law, and living a life of holiness before God. We could liken this today to various man-made religious doctrines, such as abstaining from activities like going to movies, dancing, smoking, drinking, and avoiding association with those who engage in such things.

Paul is warning that religion will creep back in, consistently attempting to alienate you from the truth of the simplicity of the gospel, which is grace apart from works. **Religion promotes the idea of Jesus plus its man-made conditions.** Many of us have encountered pastors advising us not to read certain books or avoid conferences with speakers they deem to have incorrect beliefs. The goal of religion is to confine you to the knowledge it imparts, preventing your spiritual growth by moving you away from the sphere of grace and enticing you back into the things you've been liberated from. Sometimes, it becomes necessary to distance yourself from friends still entangled in religious practices, as they can consistently attempt to pull you back into those old ways. In such situations, the best approach may be to show them love from a distance while maintaining your spiritual journey.

Paul asked if the reason he had become their enemy was for sharing the truth. He questioned whether they were listening to religious garbage that would again bring them into bondage. It still occurs today, with people breaking away from others when their beliefs diverge because religion builds fellowship around specific beliefs and doctrines. We will never have true unity of faith if we group ourselves solely based on our beliefs without a willingness to understand and accept differing perspectives.

> Avoid taking offense when friends distance themselves. I understand it can be painful, but resist the urge to be offended. Instead, let your actions reflect the love and grace you carry.

Grace serves as religion's kryptonite, and religious groups often steer clear of pure grace because of their stark opposition to it. Religious cults follow the pattern Paul described in these verses

— separating from their families when beliefs differ. This separation aims to recondition individuals, returning them to a state of bondage. It can often involve twisting verses to suit their agenda. Most of us have experienced that with such verses as 2 Thessalonians 2:1-4.

> **2 Thessalonians 2:1-4:** *"Now, brethren, concerning the coming of our Lord Jesus Christ and our gathering together to Him, we ask you, not to be soon shaken in mind or troubled, either by spirit or by word or by letter, as if from us, as though the day of Christ had come. Let no one deceive you by any means;* for *that* Day will not come *unless the falling away comes first, and the man of sin is revealed, the son of perdition, who opposes and exalts himself above all that is called God or that is worshiped, so that he sits as God in the temple of God, showing himself that he is God."*

Religion cautions against those who embrace grace and are deceiving you by claiming that these grace-loving individuals are the ones described in verse two; they are the ones who have supposedly fallen away from the rapture, from believing in a literal eternal conscious torment, and from the faith itself, including the belief in the Bible's absolute inerrancy. Religion misuses verses like this to assert that *you* have strayed from the truth when, in reality, *they* are the ones who have departed from the pure Gospel of grace.

Revelation Maturing: Growing in the Light of Grace

> **Verses 18-20:** *"But it is good to be zealous in a good thing always, and not only when I am present with you. My little children, for whom I labor in birth again until Christ is formed in you, I would like to be present with you now and to change my tone; for I have doubts about you."*

In verse 18, Paul encourages the Galatians to be zealous for grace, which is a clear indicator of freedom. These Galatians were babies (*neipos*) concerning this message of grace. A key sign of grace is the ability to remain consistent in your identity and accept others as they are, regardless of the company. Paul highlights hypocrisy in verse 18, pointing out that changing one's behavior depending on the people they're with is to be a spiritual chameleon, altering one's colors to fit the environment.

In verse 19, the solution to the back-and-forth shift between grace and religion is found in Paul's laboring until Christ is fully revealed or formed in them. While the fullness of Christ already resided in them, Paul's intention was for this inner Christ to be unveiled entirely, allowing everything He is to surface in their lives. Thus, Paul's labor or travail is focused on their full realization. Christ was indeed within them, but they hadn't reached a point in their sonship development where they could fully grasp this truth.

Colossians 2:9 says that in Jesus dwells the fullness of the Godhead bodily. Then verse 10 says, "And you are complete in Him." In Christ, that same fullness dwells within us. We can recognize its manifestation when we remain consistent in our character, regardless of the group of people we find ourselves with. We allow Him to emerge from within us.

Paul then prays for the enlightenment of our understanding so we may grasp the hope of our calling in Christ Jesus. **This process of enlightenment is gradual, unfolding over time.** As Paul matured, he realized that God's grace was sufficient, His strength is perfect in our weakness, and he quit asking God to remove the thorn in the flesh. We often pray to be relieved of things, but God may use our weaknesses to showcase His grace and strength.

In Paul's case, I believe his "thorn in the flesh" wasn't a physical ailment but the constant presence of the Judaizers. These individuals imposed legalistic interpretations on Paul's message of grace. They relentlessly harassed him, and he sought God's intervention to remove them. However, God's response affirmed that His strength shines through Paul's weaknesses. This process aimed to mature Paul to the point where he could declare, "It's no longer I who live, but Christ who lives in me." You can only reach this point when God has demonstrated His strength in every situation. Ultimately, Paul could say, "I have finished my course, I have run the race, I have kept the faith."

In his letter to the Galatians, Paul desires to assist them in shedding the burdens and constraints that weigh them down. His message to them is intended to help them establish a consistent faith. This consistency and endurance in faith are forged through the challenges posed by religious pressures. Remember, patience is remaining steadfast in the face of adversity. You truly comprehend patience when you experience pressure and learn how to maintain consistency.

That's the essence of Galatians. It guides you on a journey of maturation toward manifested sonship, where you can confidently declare, "God is good all the time, and all the time God is good!"

Chapter 11

Breaking Religious Chains: Freedom in Grace

In Galatians, the central message is the freedom from the law that comes through Christ. Paul penned this letter to guide the Galatians away from religious dependency and rituals to prevent them from reverting to the belief that they had to follow man-made rules to gain God's favor.

Law vs. Grace: An Unveiling Analogy

> **Galatians 4:21-22:** *"Tell me, you who desire to be under the law, do you not hear the law? For it is written that Abraham had two sons: the one by a bondwoman, the other by a freewoman."*

Paul begins by drawing an analogy between law and grace, freedom and bondage, using Abraham's relationships with the handmaiden Hagar and his wife Sarah.

Verse 23-25: *"But he who was of the bondwoman was born according to the flesh, and he of the freewoman through promise, which things are symbolic. For these are the two covenants: the one from Mount Sinai which gives birth to bondage, which is Hagar— for this Hagar is Mount Sinai in Arabia, and corresponds to Jerusalem which now is, and is in bondage with her children— "*

He is speaking symbolically of the two covenants, the one from Mount Sinai, which is the Law, and the Ten Commandments. It is the one who gives birth to bondage, Hagar, the handmaiden. Then, he likened Hagar to Jerusalem, the center of the Jewish religion.

Verse 26-28: *"But the Jerusalem that is from above is free which is the mother of us all. For it is written: Rejoice O barren You who do not bear! Break forth and shout You who are not in labor! For the desolate has many more children Than she who has a husband. Now we brethren as Isaac was are children of promise. But as he who was born according to the flesh then persecuted him who was born according to the Spirit, even so it is now."*

The one born a slave or brought up under the law always persecutes the one born free. We see that today, with religion persecuting those of us who are walking in liberty of grace.

> **Verse 30-31:** *"Nevertheless what does the Scripture say? 'Cast out the bondwoman and her son, for the son of the bondwoman shall not be heir with the son of the freewoman.' So then, brethren, we are not children of the bondwoman but of the free.'"*

Again, Paul is comparing freedom and bondage, the flesh and spirit, and religion and the Gospel. He's setting up this dualistic comparison and uses Hagar and Ishmael as a type of the law and the flesh activity to accomplish what God gave by promise. Remember the story of Abraham and Sarah, and God promised them when they were older that they would have a child. When Sarah heard that promise, she laughed because she knew she was past childbearing age, but God made them a promise. But as time passes, as so often happens, and we don't see the manifestation of what God has promised, we try to accomplish it by the flesh. That's what Abraham and Sarah did. He took the handmaiden Hagar, a young woman in her childbearing years, and bore a child with her. The child's name was Ishmael.

Ishmael and the Flesh: Striving vs. Trusting

So, in Paul's analogy here, he's likening Ishmael to what happens when we try to do something of the flesh using Hagar and Ishmael as a type of law and flesh activity that we enter into to try to accomplish what God has given us by promise. As we end this fourth chapter of Galatians, I want to ensure that you are free from religion and living in the grace and liberty that is yours in Christ, with no more Hagar (i.e., religious) entanglements; that there are no religious bondages still clinging to your life. If we try to fulfill the promise that God has given us — of salvation, wholeness, liberty, freedom, or anything that Jesus provided through the finished work of the cross — by a flesh activity, we produce an Ishmael.

Have you ever grown tired of waiting for a promise to be fulfilled, so you decided to take matters into your own hands? We work hard on these things, thinking we're helping God with His promise. The bottom line is this: **You'll never produce spiritual fruit through fleshly effort, no matter how hard you try.** We must walk fully in God's promises and not attach ourselves to inferior counterfeits. You may need to let go of an "Ishmael" in your life just as Abraham had to send Hagar and Ishmael away. You may need to distance yourself from things representing your self-effort rather than God's best. Even though it's difficult, don't settle for less than what God has promised. Don't settle for a religious counterfeit.

Embracing Grace: Liberation from Religious Obligation

The word "religion" comes from the Latin *religio*, meaning humans' obligation to their god. In religion, something is expected if we want blessings in return. It's the ultimate quid pro quo arrangement — we worship, allegiance, recognition, etc., to appease our god and earn divine favor.

The demands religion places on us depend on which "god" is served. It could be the pagan ritual of throwing a virgin into a volcano or our modern-day Western Evangelical practice of praying the magic prayer and asking the sky "Jesus" to come and live in our hearts. But the mentality is the same: we sense an obligation to perform certain rituals or actions so our "god" will respond favorably.

The word *religio* comes from two root words. *Re* is a prefix meaning to return, and *lagari* means to bind. It represents a return to bondage. Jesus came to free us from empty, powerless religion. He did not come to establish another institutional religion like Baptist, Catholic, or Methodist. He came to abolish man-made religion and set us free. Rather than freedom, religion demands rituals and sacrifice. It refers to this sense of duty we feel to give something to our "god" before he can bless us, revolving around the belief that humans must appease the deity through various rituals and actions. It binds us rather than liberating us. Yet we have revived the same religious bondage that Jesus destroyed.

Today, many are moving away from religion, recognizing that it leads to bondage, so they want no part of it. We are entering a new season of freedom from religious bondage all across the earth. As we come into this universal shift, we must be careful not to drag remnants of institutional religion along. The more we can cut off, the freer we become.

Religion breeds insecurity, trying to get us to a place of victory through our own effort, teaching that we attain victory through diligence and discipline so that God will bless us. But the Gospel of Grace that Paul taught says we already have the victorious life in Christ. We only need to open our eyes to what we've been freely given and live from that place.

> The critical difference is that religion locks you in endless striving, and the Gospel invites you to rest in the finished work of Jesus.

We don't need religion's shackles when we are anchored to the liberating truth of Christ. Jesus said it is the truth that sets us free. Truth is a person. His name is Jesus. He freed us completely from religious bondage.

Unlocking Freedom: Five Essential Questions

Let's explore five pivotal questions that can free from religious bondage.

1. Are you 100% assured that you are completely forgiven?

Many doubt whether God has truly forgiven them because of lingering sin consciousness. At its core, sin consciousness reveals a misunderstanding of grace, doubting the completeness of Christ's sacrifice and thinking our sins are too much for the cross to cover. This doubt often stems from believing that forgiveness must be earned, not freely given. It's crucial to grasp that God's forgiveness is 100% complete and unconditional. When Jesus declared, "It is finished," on the cross, He meant that all sins, past, present, and future, were forgiven. You don't have to earn God's forgiveness. You can only receive it.

> Recognizing the sufficiency of Christ's sacrifice allows you to rest assured that your sins are entirely forgiven, regardless of past mistakes or shortcomings.

What's often missed is that God's forgiveness is not measured or given in increments. It is independent of our asking or level of repentance. The truth is that God has already forgiven all sins, past, present, and future. The sin issue has been fully dealt with once and for all.

Through a closer look at verses like Colossians 2:13 and Hebrews 9:26, we discover that sin no longer defines us, and divine judgment tied to our sins is a relic of the past. While our actions may still carry consequences in this world, God's judgment and condemnation no longer hang over us.

Colossians 2:13: *"And you, being dead in your trespasses and the uncircumcision of your flesh, He has made alive together with Him, having forgiven you all trespasses."*

Hebrews 9:26: *"He then would have had to suffer often since the foundation of the world; but now, once at the end of the ages, He has appeared to put away sin by the sacrifice of Himself."*

Embrace your freedom and challenge any intrusive lying thought of partial forgiveness. Grasp the truth of God's unconditional and limitless grace. Rest in the finished work of Christ. Walk in the full assurance of your complete forgiveness.

2. Do you believe that you're obligated to serve the Lord?

Many individuals have grown up in religious environments that placed a heavy burden on them to serve God. This burden often led to guilt or inferiority if they didn't fulfill specific roles or obligations within the church. **Heavenly news flash: the Holy Spirit doesn't coerce us into service but leads us with love. Grace never imposes an obligation or guilt trip.** Serving Jesus is about reflecting Him and living out His love and grace in your everyday, normal lifestyle. You're not obligated to prove your love for Him through endless service; your primary responsibility is to receive and rest in His love for you. Thinking you owe Him causes burnout and cheapens His love for you.

Grace never demands of us. Serving Him is a divine privilege and a delight, not a duty. It is rooted in love. Paul recognized that he was compelled not by obligation but by the love of Christ. He realized he didn't have to balance the scales; he was moved by love. As you learn to let love lead you, you'll find that what you do for Him is not a labor but a delight, an overflow of gratitude for what He has done for you. 1 John 4:19 reminds us that we love because He first loved us. What you do for Jesus should flow from your heart as a response to His overwhelming love for you, not as a way to earn His favor. In this way, your actions will bear lasting fruit.

3. Do you see yourself as a servant instead of a son?

This question is about how you perceive your relationship with God. Viewing yourself as a servant often leads to performance anxiety and rule-following, similar to the Old Testament legalistic mindset. It causes you to believe you can never do enough to please God. On the other hand, seeing yourself as a beloved son or daughter, co-heir with Christ, is liberating. The Gospel is freedom from slavery and fear. We relate to God as beloved children, not anxious slaves. The Old Covenant Law, which demanded obedience, is gone. We live in and by grace as dearly loved sons and daughters.

4. Do you think you must overcome life's trials, or Jesus will blot your name from the Book of Life?

I was once highly fearful of standing before God in judgment, having my whole life displayed on a screen. Every thought, every intention, even if I never acted on them but only pondered them in my mind, would be laid bare for all to see. I pictured myself anxiously standing there while He meticulously reviewed my life and the dreadful thought that I might have fallen short and my name blotted out of the Book of Life.

Let's consider this: In the entire Bible, spanning 31,102 verses, only one verse in the symbolic and metaphorical book of Revelation briefly touches on the concept of blotting out names from the Book of Life. If this were a profoundly critical matter, wouldn't it have been stressed more than once? Absolutely, it would. We must let go of these ingrained religious mindsets that cause us to fear eternal separation from God if we don't constantly meet His expectations.

It's not about your actions but what Jesus has accomplished. Many think that if God isn't pleased with them, they might miss out and be eternally separated from Him.

Nothing could be further from the truth! If you haven't already, I encourage you to read my book, *Hell's Illusion*, to dig deeper into this topic. We need to break free from the lying, accusatory thought that God sits on a throne, erasing our names from His book when we mess up, only to write them back in when we repent. We must grasp what He has done for us and *as us*.

In John 16:33, Jesus said, "These things I have spoken to you, that in Me you may have peace. In the world, you will have tribulation, but be of good cheer; I have overcome the world." Jesus was our Overcomer. He overcame for us and *as us*. Paul says we were co-crucified and co-risen with Christ. It's about placing yourself in the heart of the story. What He did, He did *as you*. He took humanity into Himself, overcoming the world, the flesh, and the devil — not only for us but *as us*.

> The essential question is: Do you truly believe Jesus is the Overcomer? Victory isn't contingent on your performance or obedience; it's about the Overcomer who experienced complete victory *as you*.
>
> To be *as He is in this present world*, you need to grasp what Jesus accomplished *as you*. His victory is your victory. You are in union with the Overcomer. This is excellent news!

---

5. Do you view following Jesus primarily in terms of what you must sacrifice?

Do you believe that wholehearted commitment means relinquishing everything: your time, talents, finances, resources, and even your enjoyment? Religion has frequently depicted following Jesus as a journey of total sacrifice, making it appear highly unattractive. However, what we sometimes overlook is the concept of a divine exchange. Jesus doesn't take things from us; He enriches our lives. **Wholehearted commitment doesn't mean fearing we will lose all.** It means opening our hands to receive the treasures Jesus wants to give. Let's embrace a new perspective — one of overflowing abundance. Jesus doesn't call us to emptiness but fullness.

Let me illustrate this with a story from Luke chapter 18:

In Luke 18, a certain ruler asked Jesus how to inherit eternal life. He was asking for a checklist of things to do. Jesus responded by listing some Law-based commandments. The ruler claimed he had kept all these commandments from his youth, but Jesus wanted to show him a more deeper truth. So, He said, "One thing you lack: go, sell everything you have, give to the poor, and you will have treasures in heaven. Then come, follow me."

Now, here's where the story takes an exciting turn. The ruler had a choice: earthly treasures or treasures in heaven. He was very wealthy and couldn't fathom giving up his earthly riches. The exchange offered by Jesus was to let go of earthly treasure in exchange for treasures in heaven. It wasn't about taking from him but giving him something much better. His exchange is far greater, whether it's the exchange of His life for our life, our unrighteousness for His righteousness, etc. His exchange always benefits us.

This exchange principle runs through many aspects of our relationship with Jesus. He took our sin and gave us His righteousness. He bore our shame and gave us His glory. He endured our rejection and gave us His acceptance. He overcame for us, and we share in His victory.

Embrace the freedom from institutional religion without abandoning your faith community. Release the religious constraints that hinder your understanding of the fullness of life in Christ. Religion emphasizes actions, beliefs, and doctrines, but these can't make you perfect. Remember, the Gospel is a complete and finished work. You can't add to it.

Chapter 12

Unmasking Your True Identity

Paul's perspective in Galatians is clear: when it comes to the law, it's an all-or-nothing matter. Engaging in even a tiny portion of the law means choosing a path incompatible with grace, effectively signifying a fall from grace.

> **Galatians 5:1-11:** *"Stand fast therefore in the liberty by which Christ has made us free, and do not be entangled again with a yoke of bondage. Indeed I, Paul, say to you that if you become circumcised, Christ will profit you nothing. And I testify again to every man who becomes circumcised that he is a debtor to keep the whole law. You have become estranged from Christ, you who* attempt to *be justified by law; you have fallen from grace. For we through the Spirit eagerly wait for the hope of righteousness by faith. For in Christ Jesus neither circumcision nor uncircumcision avails*

anything, but faith working through love. You ran well. Who hindered you from obeying the truth? This persuasion does not come from Him who calls you. A little leaven leavens the whole lump. I have confidence in you, in the Lord, that you will have no other mind; but he who troubles you shall bear his judgment, whoever he is. And I, brethren, if I still preach circumcision, why do I still suffer persecution? Then the offense of the cross has ceased."

Paul says if he reverted to preaching law, he would avoid persecution because it was the scandalous message of grace that stirred opposition. If you're not being called a heretic, you may not preach a pure enough message of grace, a message of Jesus plus nothing. Those entangled in the bondage of religion often find it challenging to accept your freedom from works. It drives them crazy! But continue with boldness, sharing the truth that liberates.

Verse 12-15: *"I could wish that those who trouble you would even cut themselves off! For you, brethren, have been called to liberty; only do not use liberty as an opportunity for the flesh, but through love serve one another. For all the law is fulfilled in one word, even in this: 'You shall love your neighbor as yourself.' But if you bite and devour one another, beware lest you be consumed by one another!"*

Paul urges the Galatians to be bold and unwavering in holding onto the revelation of grace they have received. He wants them to recognize that their actions, whether they involve doing or not doing certain things, do not affect their position in Christ. Their circumcision status, whether circumcised or uncircumcised, doesn't alter their true identity. Their actions are not connected to who they are. Their identity remains intact as righteous, justified, sanctified sons and daughters of God, and no action can change that. However, if they revert to a legalistic "do to be" system, it will completely engulf them, as there's no such thing as partial adherence to the law.

Paul's fundamental message is about our identity in Christ. He knows the Galatians lack complete confidence in knowing who they are, and therefore, religious voices attempt to sway them. Therefore, he systematically encourages them to firmly grasp their origin and understand the Father's perspective regarding their identity. Once they are firmly rooted in this truth, the doubts and conflicts concerning the law and grace, as well as the external influences, will gradually fade away.

Subverting the Identity Thieves

At times, external factors can influence how you perceive yourself. These are known as "identity thieves." In our contemporary world, we're acutely aware of the importance of safeguarding our personal information and protecting against identity theft, which is the stealing of someone's true identity and personal information for dishonest purposes. Religion is similar to identity thief because it often distorts your true identity, leading you to believe you are something you're not, all for its own agenda. When religion makes you feel less than your authentic self, it hinders confident self-expression. You start believing subtle lies about who you are. This false identity, rooted in performance and others' opinions, imprisons you.

How we see ourselves must align with how the Father sees us. How does He see us? Justified, sanctified, and blameless. This is who we are apart from anything we do or don't do. Performance doesn't define us. Christ defines us. Transformation isn't about trying to change behavior or appear righteous. It starts with awakening to our rightful identity in Christ. This inner realization naturally affects our actions and lifestyle. **Genuine transformation originates from within.** God established our identity from the beginning, before the foundation of the world; no action or inaction can ever change that.

Firmly Rooted Identity: A Foundation for Purpose

> **Genesis 2:7:** *"And the LORD God formed man of the dust of the ground, and breathed into his nostrils the breath of life; and man became a living being."*

In that pivotal moment, God established humanity's eternal identity. He breathed His own breath, the breath of life, into mankind. Every time you draw a breath, every inhale, it's a reminder that you are breathing in His life. He never revoked this gift, even when Adam messed up. The breath of life, God's own essence, which He breathed into us, is the core of our identity and our origin.

As you draw each breath, remember it is His Life dwelling within you, which forms the bedrock of your identity. Your true identity has always been secure in Christ.

In Romans 11:36, Paul's proclamation that everything has its origin in God, he emphasized the understanding of God as the Source. All things flow through God, and how you navigate life is intricately connected to Him. Additionally, everything ultimately returns to God. Understanding our eternal origination allows us to comprehend our destination. What God set in motion, He also brings to a close, for He is both the Beginning and the End, the Alpha and the Omega. Since the very moment when He breathed the breath of Life into us, He asserted His ownership over us — we eternally belong to Him. Nothing we could ever do or not do would change that. There is tremendous security in that!

In Genesis 1:26, God, speaking in the plural form as Father, Son, and Holy Spirit, declared, "Let us make man in our image, according to our likeness, and let them have dominion…" God created humanity, both male and female, in His image. Verse 28 says that God blessed them and instructed them to be fruitful, multiply, fill the Earth, subdue it, and have dominion. This account in Genesis stands as the original image of humanity, the very essence of our identity that God infused in us, and it remained unaltered despite Adam's sin.

Firmly Rooted Identity: A Foundation For Purpose

You will confront challenges that seek to reshape or undermine your identity throughout your life. Consider Adam and Eve in the Garden of Eden. They encountered a temptation that caused them to question their inherent identity. They failed to believe that they were created in the image and likeness of God, infused with divine life and the breath of the Creator Himself. Something attempted to redefine their identity, suggesting that they needed to take specific actions to become like God. This theme persists in many religious teachings today, where individuals are taught that they must do something to become godly. Yet, Jesus' message is different. He proclaims that we don't need to do anything to become because we have already become.

> Our identity is not something to strive for because it's who we already are.

The tests Jesus encountered during His forty days in the wilderness were all attempts to challenge His identity, posing questions like "If you are the Son of God, turn these stones into bread." Adam and Eve faced a similar situation when they questioned, "Did God truly say this?" The Father strongly emphasizes our identity and desires it to be deeply rooted in us before He commissions us for the tasks He has called us. He first wants our view of ourselves to align with His.

Humanity's identity was defined as God's image-bearers before they were placed on earth. Identity preceded mission. Similarly, Jesus' identity was affirmed at baptism as the Father declared, "This is my beloved Son." While Christ, the Eternal Spirit, was aware of His eternal identity, Jesus in human form needed to hear this before embarking on His redemptive work. Identity empowered mission. Likewise, Paul's Damascus road encounter affirmed his identity before his ministry began. Abraham was established as the father of faith before fathering nations. Moses was revealed as Israel's deliverer at the burning bush before confronting Pharaoh. Identity precedes calling.

> Our core sense of who we are as image and likeness of God equips us for destiny.

Like these biblical figures, we operate from who God says we are, not for what we do. Our unwavering identity precedes and empowers our mission. God will firmly establish your true identity in you, aligning it with who you have always been until it becomes an essential part of who you are before you step into the purpose He has planned for you. Those plans begin to manifest as your identity becomes more firmly affixed.

Jesus solidified the identity of His disciples in John 15:15, saying, "No longer do I call you servants, for a servant does not know what his master is doing; but I have called you friends, for all things that I heard from My Father I have made known to you." He's establishing their identity as friends, elevating their status to a peer or joint-heir relationship. Everything that the Father has told Him, He's making known to them. Then, in verse 16, He says, "You did not choose Me, but I chose you and appointed you that you should go and bear fruit and *that* your fruit should remain, that whatever you ask the Father in My name He may give you." He emphasizes, "I chose you!" It is all about identity, and once that's firmly established, He sends them out, and their fruit remains.

Defending, Embracing, and Thriving in Your Identity

Paul warns of three "identity thieves" in Galatians 5, seeking to distort our identity.

1. Our identity is not formed by the opinions of other people

Aligning our self-view with God's perspective is paramount. Others may try to shape our identity, but external voices cannot alter who we are in Christ. Our identity was established by God, who knows us fully, our nature, destiny, and potential. His perspective on us is unquestionably true.

> Rather than seeking validation from family, friends, or society, we find security in how the Father sees us. Then, we can walk free from

external pressures, anchored firmly in who He says we are.

Criticism, whether about shortcomings, failures, or appearance, can be quite challenging. Consider Jesus, who endured slander, false accusations, and even claims of demonic possession. Yet, none of these affected Him. Why? Because at His baptism, the Father declared, "This is My beloved Son, in whom I am well pleased." This unwavering affirmation became the foundation of His identity, setting the course for His mission and establishing the Source of His identity before He performed any miraculous or extraordinary deeds.

Hebrews 12:3 offers encouragement when we face doubts about our identity. It reminds us to turn to Jesus, the Firstborn among many brethren, whose life reflects God's opinion of us. He never allowed the negative opinions of others to shape His identity.

In Philippians 2:5-7, Paul highlights a key principle. It emphasizes that Jesus chose humility and servanthood to reflect His true identity with God without needing external validation. When you understand and live in harmony with your true identity, the fruits of the Spirit, like love, joy, peace, and gentleness, flow naturally. Having a firm grasp of your identity shields you from being swayed by negative judgments and opinions from others.

2. Our past does not determine your identity

Thank God for that! Your past doesn't dictate your identity, a point Paul emphasized. He had a notorious and unfavorable reputation. In 1 Timothy 1:12, Paul reveals to Timothy how Jesus empowered him, even though he considered himself unworthy. He acknowledges that he played no part in it. In verse 13, Paul openly confesses his past as a blasphemer, persecutor, and arrogant man. He received mercy because he acted out of ignorance. ***Your identity isn't about your past actions; it's about who you are in Christ.***

Again, your past, whether good or bad, doesn't define you. You have no past that can hold you back because God's mercies are new every morning. What's past is past, and you can't reach the future while clinging to the past, positively or negatively. Paul gives us several passages from his own life, such as Acts 8:3, Acts 22:4, and Galatians 1:13, revealing his unsavory past. But Paul could have never written two-thirds of the New Testament if he had allowed his past to shape his future.

Paul's perspective is evident in Philippians 3:13: "Brethren, I do not count myself to have apprehended; but one thing *I do*: forgetting those things which are behind and reaching forward to those things which are ahead." His identity was not rooted in his past but in his vision and purpose. Jesus, too, never discussed his past or background. He didn't dwell on what people might have said about him growing up. His identity was simple: "If you've seen me, you've seen the Father, and the Father and I are one." Your past doesn't dictate your identity. So, stop talking about your failures, dwelling on your flaws, and telling stories about your mistakes. None of that defines you!

3. Critics do not create our identity

Critics don't shape our identity. ***Jesus never wasted His time engaging with his critics***. Don't waste your time defending yourself to those whose primary mission is to tear others apart. There's no need to engage with judgmental and critical individuals. Don't feel obliged to respond to them.

Even in the most challenging moments, such as His final days when He faced accusations, Jesus remained silent; He didn't feel compelled to respond to these charges. Likewise, we need not respond when criticized, trying to change closed minds. That path leads to wasted energy and stolen identity. Instead, we affirm what God says about us. Critics' words lose power as we grasp our identity in Christ. Their slander need not shape us. We find security in the Spirit of Truth, not fickle voices.

Watchman Nee had an insightful perspective on this. He said that when we answer our critics, we make them our judges. Criticism is dangerous and can be a destructive force, emotionally and spiritually.

Recognize "identity thieves" as anything that attempts to distort what the Father has declared about you. I've given you a few to start, but there might be more. Your identity is a gift of grace, shaped by the One who made you and breathed life into you.

> **Isaiah 43:1** provides a powerful affirmation of our identity, stating, *"But now, thus says the Lord, who created you, O Jacob, And He who formed you, O Israel: 'Fear not, for I have redeemed you; I have called you by your name; You are Mine.'" This is the essence of what Paul sought to convey to the Galatians. Our identity cannot be found in the law or any religious system that emphasizes doing to become. It is unveiled as we rest confidently in who He declares us to be and allow His truth to shape us more than any criticism or praise. Our true identity is hidden with Christ in God. We eternally belong to Him.*

CHAPTER 13

LIVING IN THE SPIRIT REALM

For many years, we've struggled to resist the allure of our physical senses, commonly called 'the flesh,' and the information they convey to our minds. Our decisions are often based on the data gathered by these senses. That's not how we were designed to live life. Paul suggests a different approach, one where we can live free from yielding to the cravings of our flesh. He proposed that by walking in the spirit, the lust of the flesh ceases to be a problem. Religion has gotten this backward, attempting to find victorious living through formulas or steps for conquering life. Paul's simple message is that if we walk in the spirit, operating from our inner being, the flesh ceases to be an obstacle.

Galatians 5:16: *"I say then: Walk in the Spirit, and you shall not fulfill the lust of the flesh."*

He elaborates on this further in verses 17 and 18.

Soul vs. Spirit: Freedom from the Law

> **Verse 17-18:** *"For the flesh lusts against the Spirit, and the Spirit against the flesh; and these are contrary to one another, so that you do not do the things that you wish. But if you are led by the Spirit, you are not under the law."*

We've often tried to guide people in behavior modification to follow the law or to please God through obedience, activity, and dedication. However, Paul's message is clear: when the Spirit leads you, you are not bound by the law. He focuses on teaching us how to walk in the Spirit because when we do, we won't give in to the desires of the flesh, and the law won't have authority over us. He continues by explaining in the following few verses that if we allow our lives to be controlled by our five physical senses and the information they convey to our minds, our decisions will lead to the manifestation of what he calls "the works of the flesh." Then, he gives us a list of some of these works.

> **Verse 19-21:** *"Now the works of the flesh are evident, which are: adultery, fornication, uncleanness, lewdness, idolatry, sorcery, hatred, contentions, jealousies, outbursts of wrath, selfish ambitions, dissensions, heresies, envy, murders, drunkenness, revelries, and the*

like; of which I tell you beforehand, just as I also told you in time past, that those who practice such things will not inherit the kingdom of God."

Let me remind you when he says that we will not inherit the Kingdom of God, he's not talking about going to heaven. The Kingdom of God is within you. He's saying that if these things rule our lives, we won't walk into the fullness of God's plans for us. We won't enjoy the inheritance that Christ died to give us. Then, he lists the fruit of the Spirit that should be reflected in our lives.

Verses 22-23: *"But the fruit of the Spirit is love, joy, peace, longsuffering, kindness, goodness, faithfulness, gentleness, self-control. Against such there is no law."*

Paul emphasizes that if you let these nine fruits of the Spirit guide your life, you won't be under the law's influence; you won't need to worry about the law. **This is how you free yourself from the burdens of the law. Where you place your attention is critical.**

Verses 24 to 25: *"And those who are Christ's have crucified the flesh with its passions and desires. If we live in the Spirit, let us also walk in the Spirit."*

In simpler terms, if you choose a lifestyle that relies on your inner self rather than your five senses and your brain's judgments based on their input, you must learn to walk in the Spirit. In verse 26, Paul advises, "Let us not become conceited, provoking one another, envying one another." This passage, covering these eleven verses, is where the rubber meets the road in our lives. It reveals that we have a significant influence on how our lives unfold. It's all about living according to the dictates of the flesh, driven by our physical senses, or living in response to our inner man, where the Spirit of God communicates with our spirit. You could put it this way: it's either a life of making choices based on what you think is wise and best for you or responding to the Father, in the Son, through the Spirit. It's a choice between decision-driven living and response-driven living.

Whichever path you decide to follow, whether you walk in the flesh or the spirit, it will yield distinct fruits. There are clear outcomes of these two lifestyles, as Paul details. He lists the consequences of living in the flesh and the positive outcomes of walking in the spirit.

> The most effective way to free yourself from the constraints of the law is by embracing the law of love, joy, peace, longsuffering, kindness, goodness, faithfulness, gentleness, and self-control. These nine fruits naturally emerge as you walk in the Spirit, and as they thrive, the religious striving becomes obsolete.

The Battle Within: Flesh vs. Spirit

How can you discern whether you live by the spirit or the flesh? Here's the critical distinction: the flesh compels you while the Spirit leads you. Being driven often induces a sense of urgency and even panic, like an inner pressure to get things done. On the other hand, being led is more like a gentle tug, a drawing toward something. You can't simultaneously live in a state of compulsion and guidance; this is the heart of the struggle between the flesh and the spirit, between making self-made choices and responding to the Spirit's leading.

In verses 24 and 25, Paul emphasizes that those who belong to Christ have decisively crucified the flesh and refuse to resurrect it. **The old man of flesh died with Christ on the cross. And it was intended to remain dead.** However, for generations, we've resurrected it and given it life and authority, which has led us to where we are today.

We are on a journey where we must choose whether to be led by the spirit or the flesh. If you have eyes to see and ears to hear, you'll notice a continuous flow of fresh revelation and insight from the Spirit. For many of us who have grown up in church, this marks a new awakening and dimension.

For many years, I lived in a state of flux, constantly shifting between my soul and spirit. Many of us in religious circles have become quite adept at it. As a pastor, when I felt the leading of the Spirit, that inner prompting conveying God's desires for the church or myself, I would act on it, but only if it also made rational sense to my mind. On the other hand, when a course of action appeared logical, made sense, and garnered approval from those around me, I would respond, bypassing my spirit's input. Subsequently, I often found myself in predicaments, and that's when I'd pray and ask God to bless my efforts, even though He hadn't initiated them to begin with.

Unveiling the Unseen Realm: A New Awakening

The dynamics of grace are reshaping all of this. Grace is awakening the sons and daughters of God to a dimension that, for the most part, remained largely hidden from our full awareness. It existed but was invisible, and we didn't see it. We weren't taught how to live in it.

Questions naturally arise as I go deeper into this unseen realm and witness things I've never seen before. I ponder the cloud of witnesses mentioned in Hebrews, those meant to support and champion us. Why does it seem like we lack a connection with them? Where are the angels who ministered to Jesus, provided food for Elijah, and orchestrated Paul's miraculous release from prison? It can't be that they've fallen silent; it's more likely that we haven't been attuned to their presence. The unseen spirit world has always existed, but we've remained oblivious. No one has guided us in developing our spiritual sensitivity.

Today, the Father, through the Son and in the Spirit, is developing our spiritual sensitivity and teaching us to live in this dimension. He's unveiling it more vividly with each passing day, and it's a journey that has been unfolding since the early days of the church.

> **Acts 2:14-17:** *"But Peter, standing up with the eleven, raised his voice and said to them, "Men of Judea and all who dwell in Jerusalem, let this be known to you, and heed my words. For these are not drunk, as you suppose, since it is only the third hour of the day. But this is what was spoken by the prophet Joel: 'And it shall come to pass in the last days, says God, That I will pour out of My Spirit on all flesh; Your sons and your daughters shall prophesy, Your young men shall see visions, Your old men shall dream dreams."*

Since then, significantly since the 1900s, when a notable shift occurred, the spiritual dimension has expanded. Today, the natural and spiritual realms are converging. We're walking in the spirit more than ever and witnessing the last days of conflicted, soul-driven spiritual living. You can't straddle both worlds; it's either soul-driven or spirit-led. We're recognizing that self-will and carnal thinking haven't truly benefited us. While they might offer short-term gains, they tend to backfire in the long run. The reality of *as He is, so are we in this present world* is on the horizon, and it's not a distant future promise to look forward to. It's here and now. It's our identity in Christ.

However, we haven't fully comprehended the magnitude of what the Father is accomplishing on Earth. Our consciousness hasn't expanded enough to grasp the extent of His work or to fathom the abundant provision and opportunities He has made available to us. But, Paul, in the fifth chapter of Galatians, discussed how we can shift from being soul-driven or flesh-led to being spirit-led. Today, there's a noticeable decrease in dependence on the intellect and a significant increase in reliance on the spirit. Excessive thinking can obstruct your spiritual hearing because it leads to a conflict that Paul described, with the flesh pulling one way and the spirit another. As you lean more toward the spirit, the need for intellectual understanding diminishes. Choosing is rooted in thought and rationalization, while spirit leading is responding and doing what we see the Father do and saying what we hear Him speak.

> First Corinthians 2:9-13 says, *"But as it is written: 'Eye has not seen, nor ear heard, Nor have entered into the heart of man The things which God has prepared for those who love Him.' But God has revealed them to us through His Spirit. For the Spirit searches all things, yes, the deep things of God. For what man knows the things of a man except the spirit of the man which is in him? Even so no one knows the things of God except the Spirit of God. Now we have received, not the spirit of the world, but the Spirit who is from God, that we might know the things that have been freely given to us by God. These things we also speak, not in words which man's wisdom teaches but which the Holy Spirit teaches, comparing spiritual things with spiritual."*

The things God has prepared for us aren't perceived through our five physical senses. To truly understand what God has freely given us, we must establish a connection from Spirit to spirit, where His Spirit imparts wisdom and understanding to our spirit. In verse 14, Paul states, "But the natural man does not receive the things of the Spirit of God, for they are foolishness to him; nor can he know them because they are spiritually discerned."

The Spirit's wisdom may seem foolish to those who think naturally. It goes beyond what our senses grasp and requires spiritual insight. Throughout our lives, we've attempted to grasp these spiritual matters through logic and reason, often leading to frustration. We oscillated between relying on our soul and spirit. If something made logical sense, we'd proceed, but if not, internal conflicts would arise. Regrettably, we missed out on many of God's good plans for us over the years due to our natural-minded, rational approach. However, as we learn to live from within, we're unlocking the capacity to perceive and engage with divine truth by responding to the Father rather than making intellectual choices.

> Seeing and hearing from the Father rises from within. It doesn't enter from without. It's an inner perception or prompting, like a gut feeling. It's the Spirit of God speaking to you from within.

We are currently in a transitional phase, where we, as a generation, are guiding others from a soul-driven mindset into a more spiritual way of living. **We are learning to listen to our spirit and follow it in every aspect of our lives, from financial decisions to entertainment choices.** When you live from within, you're free from external influences. However, there has been a blindfold that separates the spiritual realm from the physical world. In reality, this veil doesn't exist. It is our lack of awareness that creates this illusion. The veil is our unawareness.

When Jesus died, He tore the physical veil in the temple that separated the Holy of Holies, where the presence of God resided, from the rest of the world. This act made God's presence available to everyone, not just the high priest who entered the Holy of Holies once a year. The veil we experience is in our minds. It obscures, covers, and distorts our perceptions. However, this mental veil gradually diminishes when we cultivate spiritual awareness and transition from living in the soul to walking in the Spirit, becoming more acutely aware of the Presence and leading of God.

Tuning Into Divine Frequencies

We are currently in an accelerated process of this transformation. So, don't be surprised by the rapid pace of your learning and the abundance of revelation. Our personal vibrational level is ascending, and as it elevates, we become more attuned to the Spirit. We grow increasingly aware of the Spirit's presence, and our ability to hear spiritually improves.

As your spirit becomes highly developed, you'll find that you can "see" with your spirit as easily and clearly as you did with your natural eyes. The communication from the Father to His sons and daughters isn't solely through words; it's more about the transmission of energy and frequency. In spiritual communication, you tune in to the right frequency and learn to listen to the right vibrational level. It's not a verbal exchange; it's all about tuning into the correct frequencies and hearing the communication of Spirit to spirit.

Consider this analogy for a moment. Imagine the spiritual frequencies around us, much like radio frequencies. Every radio and television station is available if you're tuned into the right frequency, but you can't see them. What you need is a receiver, like a radio. When you plug it in and turn it on, it's tuned to pick up specific frequencies, be it AM, FM, or even Sirius. These frequencies are invisible but very real. You only need the right equipment to pick them up. For example, in my car, I can preset my radio to my favorite stations. In other words, I can preset it to my preferred *unseen frequencies*. With a simple turn of a knob, I can access them anytime I want. What if Jesus (with His radio being the Holy Spirit) had preset frequencies from the Father? Frequencies for healing, performing miracles, walking on water, or multiplying loaves and fish. Even though these frequencies are unseen, He could tune into them whenever needed.

Our ability to operate in the Spirit depends on our understanding of it. People perish due to a lack of knowledge, not a lack of prayer or fasting. We need to learn how to work in the Spirit, and that's what God is teaching us. He is fine-tuning our receiver, cutting out the static that made it hard for us to hear so that all we hear is the Father's voice. The Holy Spirit teaches us to access the right frequency at any time, just like Jesus did. As we leave this dichotomy of spirit and soul and let them merge together as one, our vibration rises, aligning us with the right frequency.

Our words set the frequency and raise our vibration. These words come from focused intention. God spoke with focused intention during creation, using words to bring His intentions into the physical realm; this is where many of us struggle, lose focus, and become distracted. Stay focused on your intention, and use words to speak it into reality. Our words have a creative power; they can create positive or negative outcomes. They give life to your focused intentions.

> The process is straightforward: you start with a focus, express it in words, and witness its manifestation. This process revolves around vibration and frequency.

We are co-creators, reflecting the image and likeness of God. How do we co-create? The power of life and death resides in your tongue. Words breathe life into your intentions. Many of us daydream, but we often don't maintain focus on those dreams. The key is to concentrate your attention and articulate your intentions with words until you witness the manifestation; this is what faith is all about. Faith is the substance of things hoped for and the evidence of things unseen. It remains strong, progressing from focused intention to spoken words until the manifestation occurs.

Transitioning to a New Dimension of Reality

We've entering a new unseen dimension, and it's essential to ask yourself if you're prepared for this way of living. Consider John 6:21. We might read it and think, *well, that was Jesus.* However, when we turn to 1 John 4:17, it tells us that we are meant to be like Him in this present world. That's the dimension we're transitioning into. In John 6:21, it's written, "Then they willingly received Him into the boat, and **immediately** the boat was at the land where they were going." Are you ready for that kind of extraordinary experience in your life? Imagine living in Houston, and suddenly, at the Father's prompting, you find yourself in Dallas without needing a five-hour drive. That's what happened in John 6:21. Would you like to access that frequency? Jesus could. And He said we would do greater things because He went to the Father. Some might argue, "But Don, that was Jesus." True, but My Bible says, "As He is, so are you!"

So, let's consider the life of Philip.

> **Acts 8:38-40:** *"So he commanded the chariot to stand still. And both Philip and the eunuch went down into the water, and he baptized him. Now when they came up out of the water, the Spirit of the Lord caught*

> *Philip away, so that the eunuch saw him no more; and he went on his way rejoicing. But Philip was found at Azotus. And passing through, he preached in all the cities till he came to Caesarea."*

This is Phillip! This isn't Jesus or even the well-known disciples like Peter, James, John, or Paul. Philip, who is relatively lesser-known, is the central character in these verses. We started in verse 38 but let me give you the backdrop of the story.

> Verse 26-27a reads, *"Now an angel of the Lord spoke to Philip, saying, "Arise and go toward the south along the road which goes down from Jerusalem to Gaza." This is desert. So he arose and went."*

Did Philip engage in a rational debate? Did he ask his soul if this request was reasonable or logical? No, he didn't hesitate but rose and went. He responded to the angel of the Lord. *But Don, where are these angels today? Why aren't they speaking to us clearly like they did with Phillip?* They are! We're just now learning how to tune in and hear. As I said, we weren't taught how to be spiritually sensitive in this unseen dimension.

As we move on to verses 27b-29, we see Philip again responding, this time to the Spirit of God.

> The passage reads, *"And behold, a man of Ethiopia, a eunuch of great authority under Candace the queen of the Ethiopians, who had charge of all her treasury, and had come to Jerusalem to worship, was returning. And sitting in his chariot, he was reading Isaiah the prophet. Then the Spirit said to Philip, "Go near and overtake this chariot."*

Did Philip question or express concern about approaching a stranger in this situation? No, he obeyed the Spirit's directive. The Spirit didn't provide a script for Philip to follow. It was one step at a time, beginning with going over to the eunuch. Philip complied without hesitation.

In verses 30-31, we see this Spirit-led interaction continue.

> *"So Philip ran to him, and heard him reading the prophet Isaiah, and said, 'Do you understand what you are reading?' And he said, 'How can I, unless someone guides me?' And he asked Philip to come up and sit with him."*

Philip didn't rationalize it. He didn't ask his soul if it sounded logical. He tuned into the inner frequency, letting his internal receiver search for the right station. Suddenly, the radio within him hit the correct frequency, tuning into the angelic station, and the angel provided guidance. He followed that guidance. Then, the Spirit-led station kicked in, and he was tuned into the *caught-up and teleported* station. It's about a transference of energy into words, the moving of the intent of the Father's heart into Phillip's heart. It is about an ordinary person experiencing Spirit-to-spirit communication in their inner man.

Galatians chapter 5 is Paul encouraging this spirit-led life, where your spirit takes precedence, and the influences of the soul, flesh, and law lose their grip on you. You might think some of this is crazy, but it's only perceived that way because we've been unaware of it. We haven't tuned into it. The Spirit searches the deep desires of the Father and raises our awareness to align with His intentions.

Are you prepared to embrace this dimension as your new normal? Are you ready to enter this dimension where the Father is pouring out His spirit, expanding our understanding, and leading us into the full manifestation as sons and daughters of God?

Chapter 14

Spirit Led Decision Making

Imagine standing at a crossroads, with two distinct paths stretching out before you. One is well-trodden, marked by the rules and traditions of the past. It is the path of the law. The other is less traveled, paved in the gentle rhythm of grace. It is the path of the Spirit. Just as the early Christians in Galatia faced the crossroads of legalism and grace, we, too, encounter similar dilemmas in our lives.

In this final chapter of Galatians, we'll explore Paul's urgent plea for restoration and compassion, his counsel on sowing the seeds of righteousness, and his final warning to steer clear of legalism. Then, we'll examine seven vital questions for making Spirit-led decisions that can transform your life.

Paul's Urgent Plea: Restoring Others with Compassion

> **Galatians 6:1:** *"Brethren, if a man is overtaken in any trespass, you who are spiritual restore such a one in a spirit of gentleness, considering yourself lest you also be tempted."*

Paul addresses those more spiritually attuned, reminding them that individuals will stumble, face challenges, and fall short. He lets them know that it's the responsibility of those more spiritually mature to engage in restoration rather than condemnation, judgment, or exclusion. Within the body of Christ, you can identify those with maturity and some level of spiritual understanding; they are restoring instead of judging.

He is appealing to these newly converted Christians. It's worth noting that even among them, the most spiritually mature individuals might not have been exceptionally mature. So, Paul tells them what they need to do.

> **Verses 2-5:** *"Bear one another's burdens, and so fulfill the law of Christ. For if anyone thinks himself to be something, when he is nothing, he deceives himself. But let each one examine his own work, and then he will have rejoicing in himself alone, and not in another. For each one shall bear his own load."*

In the first five verses, Paul emphasizes the importance of empathy towards those who stumble and fall back into the grip of the law or religious practices. He urges them to offer restoration and extend the same grace and love that Christ has shown them. Also, cautioning that when these individuals return, influenced by the law, they might become judgmental and may challenge the grace-based teachings. Therefore, he advises addressing this issue immediately, nipping it in the bud. Be kind, be tolerable, restore them in grace and love, and take care of your own business. Make sure your own house is in order and swept clean.

> **Verses 6-10:** *"Let him who is taught the word share in all good things with him who teaches. Do not be deceived, God is not mocked; for whatever a man sows, that he will also reap. For he who sows to his flesh will of the flesh reap corruption, but he who sows to the Spirit will of the Spirit reap everlasting life. And let us not grow weary while doing good, for in due season we shall reap if we do not lose heart. Therefore, as we have opportunity, let us do good to all, especially to those who are of the household of faith."*

Paul is like a parent leaving the house, giving important instructions to the believers in this sixth chapter. He's reminding them to be generous givers and to do what's right. It's like parents telling their kids not to let strangers in, not to use the stove, and providing contact information before they go out. Paul gives last-minute advice, emphasizing what he wants them to remember:

be generous and do what's right. He provides valuable counsel, highlighting the principle that what you sow, you reap. Sow to the flesh, and you'll reap judgment and condemnation. Sow to the spirit, and you'll reap love, patience, and joy in return.

> **Verses 11-12:** *"See with what large letters I have written to you with my own hand! As many as desire to make a good showing in the flesh, these* would *compel you to be circumcised, only that they may not suffer persecution for the cross of Christ."*

The false teachers wanted to compel circumcision and return to the Law. Their motive was avoiding persecution for the cross of Christ. Under the law, they may face ridicule for standards but not actual persecution because the offense of the cross is avoided. Grace brings potential persecution; religion brings conformity.

> **Verses 13-15:** *"For not even those who are circumcised keep the law, but they desire to have you circumcised that they may boast in your flesh. But God forbid that I should boast except in the cross of our Lord Jesus Christ, by whom the world has been crucified to me, and I to the world. For in Christ Jesus neither circumcision nor uncircumcision avails anything, but a new creation."*

The only thing that truly counts is being a new creation! So, in his closing remarks, Paul strongly advises to steer clear of legalism at all costs. He brings up some intriguing points, telling them that some want to make an outward show in the flesh and will pressure them to follow circumcision, not for the sake of the cross of Christ but to gain approval for converting someone back to the Law. He points out that even those who advocate for circumcision don't truly follow the law, highlighting the hypocrisy that the law can breed.

This same principle holds today. Legalistic churches often breed judgmental and hypocritical attitudes among their members. Why? Because the law strengthens sin.

Navigating Life's Crossroads in the Spirit

> **Verses 16-18:** *"And as many as walk according to this rule, peace and mercy be upon them, and upon the Israel of God. From now on let no one trouble me, for I bear in my body the marks of the Lord Jesus. Brethren, the grace of our Lord Jesus Christ be with your spirit. Amen."*

The entire sixth chapter is dedicated to the art of making sound and godly decisions that are prompted by your spirit, not your soul. It's about learning how to avoid falling back into the clutches of the law, which for these Galatians involved circumcision. It's about resisting the pressure from those who want to subject you to excessive restrictions. It's about choosing to be generous and helping those trapped by legalism. This chapter guides us in making decisions prompted by the Spirit rather than being influenced by our thoughts, emotions, or the information gathered through our five physical senses. True maturity lies in listening and responding from within, bypassing the soul's filtering of decisions, judgments, or the imposition of restrictions on others. The Spirit is an excellent Mentor and Guide that will lead you in the right direction.

As we embark on this journey, I want to offer some practical spirit-based guidelines to guide our decisions. I don't intend to confine you to rigid patterns or boxes. **Above all else, remember this: follow the peace within you.** The beauty is that you don't have to devise a plan. In the past, when we operated under the influence of our soul, we had to devise the plan ourselves. But when we walk in the spirit, it's not our responsibility to figure out the plan. It's God's role to reveal it to you Spirit-to-spirit and equip you to fulfill it.

Philippians 2:13 is a powerful verse, and it's refreshingly simple: "... for it is God who works in you both to will and to do for *His* good pleasure." This verse relieves you of the heavy burden of devising and executing the plan on your own. God takes the lead in implanting His will in you and providing you the capacity to carry it out. It is all about learning how to cooperate with His divine plan, aligning with His revealed will, and relying on His empowerment to see it through.

Let me give you seven questions you can ask yourself before making a significant decision. Please understand that this isn't about imposing rules; it's about sharing some insights that have helped me tune in to the Spirit's guidance and reduce past mistakes. When starting this journey, we won't always get it right, so these questions will help you improve your decision-making accuracy. They are practical aids for listening to the Spirit's guidance in your life.

Seven Vital Questions for a Purposeful Journey

1. Is this decision consistent with God's Word?

I want to emphasize that when I talk about "God's word," I'm not just referring to the written word in scripture. It also includes the words the Spirit speaks to you. Is this decision in harmony with what you sense deep within you? Proverbs 3:5-6 advises us to trust in the Lord with all our hearts and not lean on our understanding. Acknowledge Him in all our ways, and He will direct our paths.

There are a lot of passages in the Bible that give us wisdom that applies to a lot of our circumstances. But sometimes, you won't find a specific scripture for decisions like changing jobs, who to marry, or moving to a new city. The word of the Lord will come to you, not necessarily in scripture, but in your inner spirit. You can use verses like Proverbs 3:5-6 as a guide, where it says to trust Him with all your heart, not relying on your understanding, and

He will direct your path. It becomes an aid to what He is communicating from within.

Scripture contains wisdom and principles that can guide us in many situations. Psalm 119:105 says, "Your word *is* a lamp to my feet and a light to my path." Even if what you read in Scripture doesn't directly apply to your situation, meditating on it and hiding it in your heart can sensitize you to what the Holy Spirit may say.

> The Spirit's words and the written word can work together to light your path.

---

2. Is this a wise decision?

Proverbs is filled with wisdom and gives you a lot of practical advice. Proverbs 4:7 says that wisdom is the principal thing. Wisdom is the application of divine knowledge. It is taking His knowledge and applying it to your life.

When making decisions, consider the following sub-questions:

- What are the future consequences of this decision? Think beyond instant gratification. The Spirit of God will lead you. If you feel rushed and driven to make a choice, it might not be wise. The Spirit guides you. He draws and woos you. Flesh or your senses push and drive you to make a choice.
- Will this decision create debt? Avoiding unnecessary debt is a wise choice.
- Will this decision harm anyone? Consider whether it might negatively affect others.

In Ephesians 5:17, Paul advises us not to be unwise but to understand the will of the Lord. Make decisions with these principles in mind. The world often encourages choices based on what seems logical and feels good, following the tree of the knowledge of good and evil. However, we're called to renew our minds and not conform to the world's way of thinking.

> Life becomes simpler and more manageable as we respond to the Spirit of God in us.

Ultimately, consider if God is the Source of motivation behind your decisions. Is He leading you, or do you feel compelled by external factors? Seek the perfect will of God in your choices, moving beyond what is merely good or acceptable.

3. Can I honestly ask God to enable me to accomplish this?

If your conscience condemns you, it's a challenging path to walk. Acts 24:16 emphasizes that we should strive to maintain a conscience without offense toward both God and man. In other words, we should avoid coming to God with preconceived plans that might offend His conscience, leading to a guilty conscience on our part.

In 1 Timothy Chapter 1, Paul offers valuable advice to Timothy about conscience. In Verse 5, he highlights that the purpose of the commandment is love, coming from a pure heart, a good conscience, and sincere faith. It raises a crucial question: Can you honestly ask God to empower you to achieve anything that goes against a clear, good conscience?

For instance, let's consider financial difficulties. If you need money and decide to engage in a questionable get-rich-quick scheme, that's not in alignment with a clear conscience. Praying for God's blessing on such a venture won't work because it doesn't match a clean, clear conscience before God. God won't be a part of something ethically questionable.

This principle is vital for those in ministry. You might encounter people who approach you with fundraising ideas, always under the guise that they want to raise money to support your ministry or church. However, their true motivation is to line their pockets, not genuinely advance your ministry. It's crucial to be discerning and partner with endeavors that align with your good conscience before God. This way, you can seek His guidance and make decisions with a clear conscience.

4. Do I have a genuine peace about this?

Don't deceive yourself or attempt to convince yourself into a false sense of peace. Colossians 3:15 tells us to let the peace of God be the referee in our hearts. But how do you do that? You put yourself in neutral gear. You're neither pushing for it nor running away from it. Let the peace of God act as an umpire in your heart. Just like an umpire in a baseball game doesn't have preconceived ideas about whether it's a ball or a strike, you need to be impartial regarding decisions.

When you need to make a choice:

1. Don't let your excitement or desire for a project, business, relationship, or ministry override your peace.
2. Ensure that your sense of peace is strong when you pray about it.
3. Give God room to respond through peace.

Sometimes, what you want to do aligns with God's will, but the timing might be off. During these times, you won't experience peace and may feel anxious or driven; this is where the concept of a yellow light comes in. Sensing a yellow light means you should slow down, and learning to flow with it is essential. It might be frustrating because you're eager, but it's a sign that you must wait a bit. Rest assured, God always leads you in a direction for your best interest, whether it's a red, green, or yellow light. The key to walking in the Spirit is to trust Him. The more you trust, the easier it becomes to hear His guidance. Peace is a crucial element in guiding us to God's will; the critical aspect of peace is neutrality.

5. Does this decision fit who I am as a follower of Jesus?

This point is about character. Does this decision compromise my position or cast me in a negative light as a representative of Jesus? Is it consistent with who I am as a follower of God? It's not about imposing rules, regulations, or jumping through hoops, but rather, as a devoted follower of Jesus, does this choice align with my true identity?

God guides us to make decisions that help us avoid unnecessary problems stemming from our choices. His underlying principle is to keep us from situations inconsistent with our identity. For instance, decisions that lead to holding grudges or engaging in gossip and harsh criticism don't reflect who we are as followers of Christ.

The key here is to ensure that your choices align with your true character as a believer.

6. Does this choice and decision fit God's overall plan for my life?

Learn to take the long view; we're in a marathon, not a sprint. Does this decision align with the overarching plan God has for my life? You might wonder what that plan is, but it's what you're doing right now — His plan unfolds with your steps.

In other words, does this choice harmonize with God's purpose for your life? God has a unique plan for each person, and He will guide you to make decisions that fit His plan. As Proverbs tells us, we make choices, but God directs our steps. So, where you walk might not be your initial choice, but He's the One leading the way.

7. Will this decision bring honor to the Father?

Am I reflecting my respect and reverence for the Father and His choices in this significant decision? It's crucial to consider whether this decision aligns with the character of our Father, who is not characterized by anger, jealousy, vindictiveness, or retribution. Does this choice draw me closer to His likeness, or am I merely pursuing my own desires? It's important to recognize that people are observing the consistency in our choices, and we certainly don't want to appear hypocritical. As Paul warned about hypocrisy under the law, we strive to follow the Spirit and walk in the Spirit, which inherently prevents hypocrisy. Every decision should reflect our union with the Lord — we say what we hear Him say and do what we see Him do.

Consider these seven questions as your trusted companions on this journey. They're like your personal GPS for making Spirit-led decisions, helping you navigate the twists and turns of life. It's not just about making a choice; it's about making a commitment.

Think of it this way: Imagine you're a pastor, and you've received a profound revelation about grace, a truth that can transform lives. You're eager to share it with your congregation. But here's the catch: are you willing to stand by that decision, unwavering, even in the face of criticism, potential consequences, or the inevitable misunderstandings that may come your way?

Think of Noah, who embarked on the monumental task of building the ark, facing ridicule and enormous challenges. He committed to his decision despite the odds stacked against him. Imagine God revealing a new truth, a deeper understanding, something you're passionate about teaching and living. **Will you stay the course, following that revelation wherever it leads, no matter what outcome God has in store for your life?**

This is the heart of it: Spirit-led decisions are about an unwavering commitment to the path you've chosen, despite the inevitable obstacles or unexpected detours that may arise. It's a journey of profound trust, where you follow the inner prompting of the Spirit and surrender the ultimate outcomes to Him knowing He only has good in store for you!

About the Author

Don Keathley is the author of six books and President of Don Keathley Ministries and Global Grace Seminary. He is married to his wife Linda, and they have two grown and married daughters, Janell and Shawn, and four grandchildren.

Don received degrees from Olivet Nazarene University and a Ph.D. from Barnham Graduate School and Seminary. As president of Global Grace Seminary, he brings over 40 years of pastoral experience and a heart to develop leaders on the cutting edge of the message of grace and the finished work of the cross.

Also by Don Keathley

These titles can be found on Amazon

RELIGION BUSTERS

HELL'S ILLUSION

BARKING UP THE WRONG TREE

UNHOOK THE BOOK

GRACE ON STEROIDS

GOSPEL FREE FROM DOCTRINES

To contact Don Keathley please visit www.donkeathley.com

Made in United States
Orlando, FL
08 December 2023